Wh

Shor Shamanic Epic Folktales

In another time, storytellers were vital links in our cultural continuity. These wisdom-keepers learned hundreds of tales verbatim to be passed forward. They were the libraries in whom all vital history, medicine lore, survival methods and ethical codes were conserved. Their stories were preserved so accurately that untold generations could rely on them for essential guidance.

Every folk tale holds a piece of the larger truth of our humanity. Yet, seduced by the lure of immediate information, we are leaving these stories to wither, untold, into oblivion. Thankfully, the Shor tales beautifully embraced by this volume will remain–safeguarded for a time we may need their wisdom again.

Evelyn C. Rysdyk, Shamanic teacher/speaker and author of *The Norse Shaman*, and *Spirit Walking: A Course In Shamanic Power*

In recent years the world has come to appreciate the wisdom and teachings of ancient cultures, ones that have created local economies that for thousands of years have themselves been renewable resources. The Shor are such a people. Their numbers are declining rapidly, as is their language. This amazing book is a huge step in preserving their knowledge and sharing it with a world that needs it more than ever before. Purchase this book, support these incredible people, and gain remarkable insights about living on this sacred Earth.

John Perkins, *NY Times* bestselling author of *Confessions of an Economic Hit Man* and author of five books on indigenous shamanism

Kaichi traditional storytellers were the keepers of tales that traversed vast spiritual, natural, and psychological landscapes.

The legends and characters come alive through the teller. The stories in this book represent the living record of ancient people. They carry transformative potential for the modern reader.

Llyn Roberts, MA, award winning author of *Shapeshifting into Higher Consciousness*, *Speaking with Nature* coauthored with Sandra Ingerman, and *Shamanic Reiki*

Shor Shamanic
Epic Folktales

Shor Shamanic Epic Folktales

Alexander and Luba Arbachakov

Winchester, UK
Washington, USA

First published by Moon Books, 2019
Moon Books is an imprint of John Hunt Publishing Ltd., No. 3 East Street, Alresford
Hampshire SO24 9EE, UK
office1@jhpbooks.net
www.johnhuntpublishing.com
www.moon-books.net

For distributor details and how to order please visit the 'Ordering' section on our website.

ISBN: 978 1 78904 006 7
978 1 78904 007 4 (ebook)
Library of Congress Control Number: 2017963337

A CIP catalogue record for this book is available from the British Library.

Design: Stuart Davies

Printed and bound by CPI Group (UK) Ltd, Croydon, CR0 4YY, UK
US: Printed and bound by Edwards Brothers Malloy 15200 NBN Way #B, Blue Ridge Summit,
PA 17214, USA

Also by Alexander and Luba Arbachakov

The Last of the Shor Shamans
978-1-84694-127-6

We operate a distinctive and ethical publishing philosophy in
all areas of our business, from our global network of authors to
production and worldwide distribution.

Contents

Translator's Note

Although there are approximately 12,000 Shor people living in Siberia today, perhaps 1,000 still speak the Shor language fluently. These two epic poems were originally performed in Shor, transcribed, translated into Russian by Lyubov Arbachakova, and then translated into English by Jennifer Castner in consultation with Lyubov Arbachakova. Although having an intermediary language is not always desirable for translation, the simple, repetitive, and economical language used by Tannagashev leaves less room for distortion than might be the case with a different speaker. Transliteration of Shor words into English follows a consistent pattern except where minor adjustments ease pronunciation.

About the Translator

Jennifer Castner has a Bachelor of Arts in Russian Language and Linguistics from Bryn Mawr College. She has worked as a translator and interpreter for 18 years and is also the director of The Altai Project, a nonprofit organization supporting grassroots environmental conservation and indigenous rights initiatives in southern Siberia. She has traveled extensively in Russia and Ukraine over the last 25 years.

The compilation of these materials by the Arbachakovs and translation by Jennifer Castner were funded and facilitated by the *Olympic Mountain EarthWisdom Circle*, eomec.org

Introduction

Bill Pfeiffer and I had landed in Moscow. New York City was half a world away. The next day we would be in Siberia.

Bill and I met while I was working with a nonprofit that brought North Americans and Europeans to learn from indigenous people in the Amazon Basin and Andean mountains. Bill had, for many years, been working to create liaisons with US, and Siberian environmentalists. After repeated dreams about Siberia, I'd asked Bill to help me extend the work to this part of the world that was so familiar to him. He was ecstatic to join me.

After flying from Moscow to Novekuznetsk, I took my first steps onto Siberian soil. I had entered the remote lands of my dreams.

A short, train-ride later, Bill and I were in the Shorsky town of Tashtagol where Alexander and Luba Arbachakov, the compilers of this book, welcomed us to their homelands.

The Mountains Shoria are snow-covered seven months of the year. They are known for the fir-aspen taigas (boreal forests) that appear as a blue haze against the range flanked by river valleys that boast pristine rushing waters. The Shor peaks that rise to almost 7,000 feet are part of the mystical Altai Mountain range.

Environmentalist and photographer, Alexander, and his artist and ethnographer wife, Luba, are native Shor – they are part of the mystery, legend and history of this magical, natural setting that I am honored to have visited, which comes to life through the Shor heroic tales presented in this book.

Journeys such as the epics you will find on these pages are fragments of an ancient culture. Traditionally held by *kaichi* 'storytellers', these rare stories survive the dissolution of the art of oral storytelling. It is the world's good fortune that the Arbachakovs had the foresight to record Vladimir Egorovich Tannagashev's oral transmissions before he died in 2007.

Kaichi storytellers such as Tannagashev were the keepers of epics that traversed vast spiritual, natural, and psychological landscapes. The legends and characters come alive through the teller's experience, as they are being depicted.

Story is the living record of an ancient people. It also carries transformative potential for the teller, listener and reader.

I am deeply moved in knowing these heroic tales are preserved for future generations of Shorsky children. I am delighted that through this publishing effort they are now also available to an international audience.

Llyn Roberts, MA

February 19, 2018

Heroic Tales of the Shor People as Performed by V. E. Tannagashev

The Shor are a small indigenous minority people in southern Siberia occupying southern Kemerovo Oblast. According to the 2010 census, their population numbers 12,888. The Shor language belongs to the Khakass subgroup of the Uyghur-Oguz group of Turkic languages.

The largest and most · long-standing genre of Shor folklore is алыптыг ныбак or кай ныбак – heroic (bogatyr) tales, often performed in throat-singing accompanied by the 2-stringed *kai-komus* (mouth harp). Performers of this genre are known as *kaichi* (storyteller). Recitative performers of these epic poems are known as *nybakchy* (storyteller, tale-teller).

Storytellers described performances of these heroic tales in a variety of ways: ныбак ыс-перерге ('to send off a story'); ныбак ыс-перерге ('set down a story'); кайлап-перерге ('perform *kai*'); шерт-перерге ('to unleash'). These terms testify to the people's connection to the story as something tangible, corporeal, animate.

Generally, Shor heroic tales were performed at home in the evening or at night. They not only served as a relaxing activity for people, influencing their spiritual peace, but also served a magical role, protecting them from evil spirits. It was for this reason that hunters took storytellers along on hunts, where their performances brought joy to the surrounding spirits in the forest, mountains, and rivers (таг ээзи, суг ээзи), as well as brightening the challenges of life in the taiga forest.

Unfortunately, the living storyteller tradition is gradually being extinguished among Siberian indigenous peoples. Despite this, between 1996 and 2003, we were able to make audio and video recordings of 27 epic hero tales performed by the well-known Shor *kaichi* Vladimir Egorovich Tannagashev (1932-2007) in both recitative and throat-singing (accompanied by the 2-stringed *kai-komus*) forms.

Tannagashev knew about Shor *kai* from his early childhood, listening to performances by well-known period Shor storytellers Moroshko (N. A. Napazakov) and Akmet (A. I. Abakaev) who lived in other villages in the mountainous Shor lands. He was also familiar with the epic tales told by P. I. Kydyyakov, S. S. Torobokova, P. N. Amzorov, and many others. He considered, however, his teacher to be Prokopy Nikanorovich Amzorov, in whose footsteps he followed, playing on the balalaika. Beginning in his thirties, Tannagashev performed tales for friends and family, and later he began to be invited to funerals, where he was asked to perform epic poems with tragic endings throughout the night.

This author's acquaintance with Tannagashev began in 1996 in his apartment. We determined that he remembers approximately 80 hero poems, generally performed in the чоокпа style ("speaking, speech"), that is, recitative. Upon our request, he performed several tales in throat-singing *kai* with the accompaniment of the 2-stringed mouth harp.

In performing these pieces, Tannagashev does not deviate from established tradition. Like other storytellers, he "is present" in the epic world, accompanying the *bogatyr*[1] on his journey: *"Вроде мен ыларба парчам"* / "It was as if I set off with them." For example, narrating the adventures of the protagonist of the tale "Svet Olak", Tannagashev said: "А мен Свет Оолакпа полбодурчам". / "But I will remain here with Svet Olak."

N. P. Dyrenkova was the first to discuss the ability of the *kaichi* to delve into the virtual life of the hero, mentally accompany the hero on the journey, and then convey the events to listeners as a direct observer during performances of epic poetry. She cites the example of one storyteller who said: *"Мееҥ сағыжым ныбақ чолу-ба парды."* / "My mind went along the way of the tale." Shor folklore researcher A. I. Chudoyakov also noted the skill of the *kaichi* to "mentally see" the path of the bogatyr.

It is important to note that the concept of "path" or "way of the bogatyr" includes the "bogatyr biography" of the hero as a component of the storytelling itself. As with all other Turkic and Mongolian peoples, Shor performance ritual prevents the storyteller from abandoning the hero along the way. In other words, once the bogatyr's tale is begun, the storyteller must bring the story to its logical conclusion without omitting a single detail. Tannagashev followed this rule as well, in observance of epic tradition.

The *kaichi* announces his presence within the epic story over the course of events as well as at their conclusion. At the outset, the storyteller conveys his vision of the world in the first person as an introduction for listeners. His interest in the tale, personal greeting of the bogatyr, and emotionally colored speech are all reflected in the flow of the events: "Эжик аш, эзен перчам, / Поза алтап, менчи перчам. / Анаӈ кӧрбодурғаным." "Having opened the door, he made greeting, / Crossing the threshold, he bowed. / Then, I see...."

During the remainder of the story, the narrator's voice vanishes, appearing only in descriptions of the bogatyr's lengthy journey. In those cases, the *kaichi* reminds listeners of his function – to tell the story: "Мен айдарға табрақ полча, / Ол нанарға керим пол-бодурча." "I can tell it quickly, / While a long journey awaits him." ("Kyun Kёk")

There are similar remarks in other stories, for example, the story of "Altyn Syryk", recorded by A. I. Chudoyakov.

*   *   *

The stories published here, *Chepe Salgyn with the Plain Brown Horse* (Чеппе сар аттыг Чеппе Салғын, recorded in January 1997) and *Kёk Torchuk* (Кӧк Торчук, recorded in April 2001) were recorded using L. N. Arbachakov's voice recorder and performed by V. E. Tannagashev, a representative of the Mrassu epic poem tradition.

These hero stories were performed by the *kaichi* using a variety of techniques: *Chepe Salgyn with the Plain Brown Horse* in the traditional oral style (recitative) and *Kёk Torchuk* using throat singing accompanied by the 2-stringed *kai-komus*.

The performances took place following epic tradition. However, because of the oral nature of storytelling and the *kaichi's* good command of epic poetry style, he was relatively freewheeling. Improvisation depends to a large degree on the performer's mastery, his in-depth knowledge of the entire foundation of poetic resources, and the structural laws of hero stories, and this was well demonstrated by the storyteller in the texts we selected for publication.

Moreover, further study showed that modern-day educated storytellers may borrow scenes from Russian literature. For example in the story *Chepe Salgyn...*, after the representatives of the Lower World (Older-Younger Ches Shemeldei) had stuffed the hero into the iron barrel, "they sealed it with the lid, / and pushed it into the black sea" ("Тебир бочкее кире суккелип, / Қалпағын чапкелип, / Қара талайға ийдибистилер"). It is possible that this scene was borrowed from A. S. Pushkin's "Tale of the Tsar Saltan", in which the heroine and her son, sealed in a barrel, are dropped into the sea. It seems to us that in this case, in the place of the barrel a raft should have been used – a more traditional floatation device for the Shor.

In *Kёk Torchuk*, Tannagashev himself reports that he created the fight scene in which the antagonists threatening the life of the protagonist are dragged under into the Underworld by a hand reaching up from under the earth and belonging to a dead bogatyr who had not yet reached the place "where souls die". Already in the Underworld, this "dead *alyp*" fighting with opponents destroys them and then departs to the world of the dead forever.

The main theme of the two tales is a struggle with an invader. In the stories, the attack on the bogatyr's land is due to the desire of the enemy to take possession of many cattle and other wealth, as well as the khan's subjects and his large territory. Themes of the epic protagonist's protection of the property of a powerless, aging *alyp* from the attacker, subsequent freeing of the people, and a protest against violence are all clearly reflected in these tales.

Another important topic highlighted in the selected stories is heroic matchmaking and the journey to reach one's bride. This theme is found widely in the epic poetry of the Altai-Sayan peoples (Shor, Altaian, Khakass, Tuvan). S. S. Surazakov wrote that in early Altaian epic poetry acquisition of the bride became a generic heroic feat.

Despite the differences in plot, these two tales share the artistic-performance and stylistic resources and techniques common to all Shor epic poetry. Most of all, this relates to "common places" and other poetic descriptions characteristic of this folklore genre. These include: creation stories, appearance of the *alyp*, bogatyr feasts, the psychological state of the hero (rage, terror), running horses, bogatyr travel, description of the passage of time and space, length of the journey, theft of livestock and people, dueling and duration of *alyps'* battles, appearance of the bride, wedding feast, beginning and end, and addressing the listeners.

At the same time, each tale contains its own specific (situational) places and epic formulations. For example, in the tale *Kёk Torchuk* the *kaichi* addresses his only listener-storygatherer, "sharing" the success of the khan, while in *Chepe Salgyn...*, there is no such moment of connection.

In the story *Chepe Salgyn...*, the main heroine and protector of hearth and home and her father's possession is a girl – Altyn Chustuk, with enormous breasts that are compared to mountains ("пир эмчеги пир тайғачы"). She battles the strongest opponent, the girl Kydai Aryg, who arrived on an iron raft laid across nine pairs of light chestnut horses: "тоғус пара ай кор аттыҥ ӱстӱнге тебир сал иштетиркел, салтырсалған полтур." It turns out that the girl Kydai Aryg, having arrived on nine pairs of horses, has forty breasts: "кырық эмчектиг / Қыдай Арығ кирча." Chudoyakov recorded a different version of "Қырық эмчектиг Кудай Арығ" in 1968, when it was performed by N. M. Akulyakov and he noted that "in this story, the Forty-breasted Kydai Aryg first appears in the role of Kara Shemeldei... Beginning in the middle of the poem, she acquires new qualities, different from all the other negative female figures. She becomes fertile...." In our tale, Kydai Aryg, assigned the epithet of "кырық эмчектиг" ('forty-breasted'), dies in a battle with the bogatyrka Altyn Chustuk, without bearing offspring. Later, Altyn Chustuk, reincarnated by the *chaiachi*-creator as a bogatyr-man named Chepe Salgyn, defeats Kara Alyp and, having married his betrothed, returns with her to his lands. However, he must still face a series of trials: captivity and battles with inhabitants of the Underworld, the Kara Shemeldei demons.

The conflict, the set-up event in Kĕk Torchuk, arises at the moment that Kĕk Kan's lands are attacked by an invader whose goal is to enslave the khan's people and steal his livestock. At the time of the elderly Kĕk Kan's death, a child comes to his aid, appearing from a magic egg planted by the sole creator-*chaiachi*.

Usually, a newborn child is sent off on a distant and dangerous journey only after undergoing a naming ritual. In *Kĕk Torchuk*, the boy, as yet unnamed, deals with the invader and immediately decides to continue onward in order to destroy all of the khan-invaders as well as the *alyps* of the Underworld. At the tale's end, he returns home with his bride and, together with his parents, they celebrate a rich wedding.

Along with tales of heroic deeds, the subject matter of the two tales includes many mythological aspects (motifs, characters). For example, in *Chepe Salgyn...* an 'iron swallow' (тебир карлык) delivers an 'urgent letter' (сабыр мичик кат) to the girl Altyn Chustuk from the sole creator-*chaiachi*. The same legend tells of a black bogatyr by the name of Kara Alyp who was created by nine creators: "Э, четтон алыптың кӱжӱ / Қара тайғадаң чайалган / Қара Алып полтур-но!..." 'Eh, it was Kara Alyp, made from the black mountain, / With the strength of seventy *alyps!*...'

In epic poetry, bogatyrs enter the Underworld, generally occupied by antagonists, in a particular way: they travel through a special entrance-*tyundyuk* (чер тӱндӱги), where 'tyundyuk' is the term for the opening in the roof of a yurt or ger. Generally speaking, characters in *Chepe Salgyn...* can live anywhere, for example, inside mountains. Thus the parents of Chepe Salgyn's bride live 'inside an iron mountain' (тебир тайға иштинге). Interestingly, the same sun and moon shine there: "пок күн, пок ай шалча."

It is known that the *alyps* of the Underworld possess unusual objects. In *Chepe Salgyn*..., the Ches Shemeldei use a 'rawhide strap' (чаш қайыш) as a weapon. In addition to weapons, the tales mention a variety of magical items, including a 'golden book' (алтын книга) describing the fate of a person.

The miraculous transformation of people and animals in *Chepe Salgyn*... usually occurs after a simple ritual. For example, the protagonist Chepe Salgyn is turned from a girl into a male bogatyr following a naming ceremony conducted by the sole creator. Having received a name and then falling deeply asleep, she awakens as a male bogatyr '[the size of] a mountain' (тайға шени алып пол партыр).

Chepe Salgyn can also perform miracles: upon seeing three girls battling with *alyps*, he created a twin of himself and a horse out of his own hair and dispatched them to the place of the bogatyrs' battle: 'When he pulled the three hairs, / And thrice spitting phlegm on them, he tossed them – / A different plain chestnut horse appeared. / He took the plain chestnut horse by the reins, / Another Chepe Salgyn appeared.' ("Үш кулған шаш шура тартыпкелип, / ӱш када кағыркел, тӱккӱркел, таштабыза пергени: / Чеппе сар ат тура сергиде. / Чеппе сар аттың чедингенче /Чеппе Салғын тура сергиде."). Following a lengthy combat, the *alyps* destroy their opponents, usually by striking them on a stone: "...A black stone / That looked larger than a cow: / Kara Kan Mergen's backbone / Broke apart into nine pieces." (...нектең улуг / Қара ташты көркелип, /Тӱжӱрӱбӱзе пергени: / Сын ортқазын тоғус чердең / Сыы шапкелип, тӱжӱрӱбӱсти.) (From *Kёk Torchuk*)

Some of Tannagashev's tales contain unusual comparisons. For example, in *Kёk Torchuk*, when describing the temperamental character of an *alyp*, the storyteller uses natural objects such as a roiling or roaring sea: "A single one of his eyes / Was like a roiling white sea. / The other eye / Was like a roaring black sea!" ("Пир карағыннаң ак талай / Толкуп акчыған ошкаш, / Пир каранын

9

қара талай / Толкуп акчыған ошқаш!").

More traditional descriptions containing common and formulaic expressions also occur, as in *Chepe Salgyn…*: "Having survived to the third generation…" (Ӱш тӧлге чеде-берген….). Sometimes this formula can be combined with another enduring cliché used to describe the protagonist: "Who filled the white world with his birth" ("Ак чарыкка толдура туған"). There is another regular and noteworthy character in Shor epic poetry: the golden cuckoo. In Shor hero tales, golden cuckoos bring news of battles between horses and play an important role in the pre-marriage ritual of fighting for the bride. Here is an example from *Kёk Torchuk*: "From the height of forty heavens / The golden cuckoo began to sing: / – Alyps, what are you doing / Sitting there in the golden palace? / The horses are already returning! – the bird cuckooed." ("Ӱстӱнгӱзе кырык тегри ӱстӱнде /Алтын кӧӧк кел кӧглепча: / – Алтын ӧргеде алыптар, – тедир,– / Абаларың иштеп, одурчазар ба? / Аттар қалғаны айланышчар.")

In another of Tannagashev's tales, *Older Brother and the Chestnut Roan Horse with Younger Brother and the Chestnut Horse*, the cuckoo announces the birth of the bogatyr's horse. Thus, in epic poems, this bird character assumes the role of herald regarding fateful events in the epic world.

In *Kёk Torchuk*, Tannagashev used rare figurative expressions such as: "I would close my chokecherry eyes / I would lay down my head, my egg…" ("Ныбырт кӧзӱм мӱнерим, / Ныбыртка пажым саларым"). The same such poetic turns of phrase are found in the tale *Kyuyush Kan* by *kaichi*-storyteller and poet S. S. Torobokov.

'Entrance of the bride' is also a traditional event in epic poems: "The girl came out, attended by sixty servants, / With seventy retainers – / And the golden palace was lit up with red light." ("Алтон қожанчыба, / Четтон паранчыба пас шықты қыс палазы. /Алтын ӧрге кызара ноо, сустап парды.") (*Kёk Torchuk*).

Shor hero epics contain an intrinsically well-developed system of artistic-stylistic devices (hyperbole, synonyms, allegory, metaphor) that permit particular creativity in the created world's poetic imagery. Even the characters' names are given defining characteristics: "Kuba Salgyn, / The immortal, undying, / Who filled the world with his birth!" ("Ак чарыкка толдура туған öлбес-парбас") (*Kёk Torchuk*) and "black thoughts" ("Қара сағыштығ").

Such epithets facilitate the description of an idealized hero and an idealized environment in which epic characters appear (golden, silver tables, palaces, weapons, clothing, decoration, dishes, etc.). Special mention should be made of the regular use of the descriptive phrase 'pure soul' (арығ тыны). According to Shor worldview, each living creature has a pure soul at birth. When the epic character (protagonist or antagonist) dies, his or her "pure soul leaves the body" ("арығ тыны ээде шыккан").

Kaichi often use compound names in descriptions of *alyps* and their horses: "The immortal, undying, / And strength unknowing *alyp*' (кÿжÿн пилинмес, öлбес-парбас); '...dressed in a nine-layered golden hauberk / Made with fish scales." ("...тоғус кадыл палық кастрыктығ алтын куйак кессалтыр"), "A wonderful three-eared blue-grey horse, transcending other horses," ("...аттаң артық ÿш кулактығ кöк пор ат"); "transcending other *alyps*" ("артық чайалған алып"); and "...Kёk Torchuk was born foolish!" ("алығ туған Кöк Торчук полтырым").

Tales are enriched with stylistic expressiveness using <u>paired words</u> – "undying-immortal" ("öлбес-парбас"), "under the moon-sun" ("айға-кÿнге"), <u>metaphoric names</u> – "his ears, tiring of waiting, seemed to hear the cuckoo begin to sing" ("Чапсактың кулағынға / Кööк какканче пилдирди.") (*Chepe Salgyn...*); and <u>paired comparisons</u>: "When a bad dog bites, / When a rabid cow began to butt its horns" ("Чабал адай шени капча,/Чабал нек шени сÿсча.") (*Kёk Torchuk*)

The most commonly used metaphor used in the storytelling is "clung like a bat" ("чарғанат шени кел чапшынды"), or, literally, 'stuck', evoking the imagery of a rider seemingly melded to his horse.

Hyperbolic and complicated metaphors are used to describe the beauty of girl-brides and their chosen ones, "Their beauty darkened the moon, / And beyond that the sun was eclipsed." ("Ааларыңнан ай чапшырып, / Соонаң күн чапшыр"), or in order to underscore the power of the *alyp* and his horse: "Eh, as big as a block of mountain, the *alyp* sits." ("*Э, кезек тайға шени алып одурсалтыр*") (*Kёk Torchuk*).

All scenes wherein the hero battles an attacker are based on contrasting opposing aspects of the characters. An *alyp* of the Middleworld is described as "transcendently born" ("артық чайалған"), born not only with the strength of a bogatyr but also a sense of justice. He does not share the cunning of the Underworld *alyps*, usually negatively described, for example, "having lost [their] name" ("ады читкен").

Quantitative hyperbole also plays an important role in epic poetics: "the alyp has a nine-layered hauberk", bogatyrs lift their enemies "to the forty heavens", descend to the underground world "beyond seventy layers of earth", and heroes overcome mountains "with sixty, seventy, ninety passes", and weddings are celebrated "for seven/nine days" or "with no attention to day or night."

The language of epic tales is enriched by the inclusion of good wishes, proverbs, and sayings. For example: "A roe deer that is fated to die / dashed across the snow!" ("Öлер кийик / Қар ÿстÿбе позу чÿгÿркелчең!"); or "Let your soul travel high! / Let your life's path be long!" ("Чайанның мöзÿк ползун, / Чажын узак ползун!") (*Kёk Torchuk*).

To our view, the endings of epic tales contain an inherent belief in some sort of magic. The conclusion of *Kёk Torchuk* can be divided into three parts. The first is dedicated to parting ways with the horse: "– *Eze*, blue-grey horse of mine, – he said, – / Go to the foot of Mount Syurgyu, / And, nibble three times, eat the grass! / Go to the shores of the milky lake, / And with three swallows, drink water!" ("Эзе, кöк пор ат, – *тедир*,–/ *Сÿргÿ тайға тöзинге паркелип,– тедир,–/ Ÿш кылғаннапкелип, от отта!– тедир.–/ Сÿт кöлдең*

кажынға паркелип, / Ноо, ӱш ортамнеп суг ижибодур. ")
The second part describes a ceremony for entering one's home: after bidding the horse farewell, the *alyp* enters the palace: "He turned away, / And went into the golden palace" ("Айланкелип,/Алтын öргеге кире пастыр кирди.") The recording of *Altyn Syryk* made by A. I. Chudoyakov describes the bogatyr entering the building and removing his armor and closing the door tightly.

With these actions, the *alyp* concludes the epic story, and from there the *kaichi* returns the hero to the real world using a typical formulaic expression: "In their land / No strange bogatyrs enter with a cry, / War does not occur, nor oppression. / He became a great khan of khans, / He became a great *piy*-leader among *piys*, / He lived here." ("Пылардың черге паза / Қыйғыркелип, эр кирбенча. / Қынапкелип, шериг кирбенча. / Қааның улуғ каан полуп, / Пейдең улуғ пей полкелип, / Кел чажап чатчалар." (*Kёk Torchuk*).

In the third and final part, the storyteller addresses the audience with gratitude and a blessing, especially those listeners, he says with humor, that "sat" and listened to him, or, in other words, did not fall asleep during the telling.

In the recordings by N. P. Dyrenkova and A. I. Chudoyakov (made at a time when epic poetry was still thriving), more elaborate endings were used in which the *kaichi* divides the good luck of the khan among his listeners. According to tradition, he provides it in bags strapped onto a white (sometimes black) rabbit. This is the ending we encounter with Tannagashev in the story *Kёk Torchuk*: "Lyubasha, who listened to me, / Let your soul travel high! / Let your life's path be long! / I went into the bushes, / I caught a white rabbit. / I loaded the good fortune of the white khan / Onto the white rabbit as it went here and there / I mounted the white rabbit, / And rode him to this land." ("Мени одур уккан Любаша, / Чайанның мӧзӱк ползун, / Чажын узак ползун! / Арал каштап парып, / Ақ койанак туттым. / Улуғ қааның қастағын / Ақ койанға арта-перте таштап, / Ақ койанға мӱнкелип, / По черге қачыр кирдим.")

Here, the storyteller speaks from his own perspective, apologizing (not so much to the listeners, but to the spirits of the *kai*), saying: "In telling the long tale – I did not lengthen, / In telling it briefly – I did not abridge," ("Узун теп, узурбадым,/ Қысқа теп, қызарбадым."). With these words, the *kaichi* affirms that he performed the tale and strictly observed epic tradition.

The end of the tale *Chepe Salgyn...*" was performed briefly. Apparently, it depended not only on the *kaichi*'s manner of storytelling but also on his mood. Moreover, it is possible that the gradual decline of epic tradition also influences storytelling form. As a result, epic poetry retains its compositional form while its contents and poetics are losing artistic detail.

The immediate presence of the storyteller within the epic story as a narrator-commentator, as well as a participant in the events and a traveling companion for the bogatyr himself is important not only for him but also for listeners. The *kaichi*'s magical function, given to him by spirit-helpers, allows him to serve as a guide between real and mythical worlds, providing the epic tale convincing and emotional content.

As has already been noted in Turkic literature, the structure of epic poetry is a syllabic system. Rhythmic units tend to be 7-8 syllables in length and comprise the majority of verses. Sometimes there are as many as 14 syllables. Poems do not have strict meter in terms of their intonation and declamation. The rhythmic structure of Shor epic poetry has not yet been studied and requires comprehensive and in-depth study.

The prevalence of rhythmic and syntactic parallelisms is noteworthy, as is the initial and internal alliteration and repetition.

The analysis of these epic poems performed by V. E. Tannagashev shows them to be typical examples of the Shor epic genre. They have particular artistic value as well.

* * *

During preparation of these Shor texts for publication, we have retained all misstatements, repetitions, and hesitations in the storyteller's speech as a result of oral epic storytelling. The translation (Shor to Russian)[2] took these corrections into account and made adjustments for Russian grammar and syntax.

The Russian translation of these poems includes words deeply entrenched in the Shor language (Siberian) elders: *alyp* ('bogatyr', 'hero warrior'), *churt* ('settlement'). Some words have been left untranslated in order to reflect the Shor worldview and people's traditional ways of living. For example, *toi* ('holiday', 'wedding'). In some cases other words also remain: *chaiachi, kudai* (names of upper gods, creators) that better reflect the spiritual understanding of the Shor people than the Russian versions ('creator', 'god'). Their definitions are provided in the glossary and list of characters.

In the Shor text, other speech is always accompanied by the verbal prefix '*te-*' meaning 'to say, speak' in the required grammatical form (*tep, tedir*). In essence, this verb serves more than just to convey direct speech, but rather it indicates a completed act of speech, highlights speech by characters, and separates the speech of others from the author's words. In order to indicate the character and means of speaking in the Russian text, we varied the translation of this word, replacing it instead with Russian synonyms and other verbs indicating speech.

In certain cases, the oft repeated *tedir* 'said, spoke' is omitted from the translation as is the untranslatable filler word ноо (/nō/), used by storytellers during slight pauses and often interrupting the artistic-poetic integrity of the narrative. Mentions of characters and their names are also often assumed by the storyteller rather than directly introduced into the Russian text.

The translation of *Kёk Torchuk* omits one repeated scene in the *alyp*'s journey. It occurred, according to the storyteller, when he "leapt ahead", forgetting to tell about an encounter between the main protagonist with a horse and about the written message from the sole creator regarding the *alyp*'s name.

Tannagashev's own language includes frequent loan words from

Russian, including пара ('pair'), *только* ('only'), *книга* ('book'), *все равно* ('nevertheless'), *бочка* ('barrel') and others. They can be used in these Shor grammatical forms: устол+ға 'on the table', қарманың+наң 'out of the pocket', ботинка+ның 'belonging to the boot', курва+лар+ы 'whore'. The Russian translation generally preserved Shor and Russian prepositions, particles, conjunctions, interjections, and modals (а, э, о, ээ, ноо,не, обо, хе, аданмада, оғо, но-ка, ок), underscoring the oral nature of folkloric text. They help the performer to react emotionally to epic events or, upon stumbling, to recall a particular episode in the narrative.

I would like to express my enormous gratitude to V. M. Telyakova who edited the Russian texts, providing valuable commentary to both the translations and the glossaries.

Lyubov Arbachakova

V. E. Tannagashev

Kёk Torchuk

-1-

Before today's generation
After the long-ago generation.
It was in the time,
That the earth was taking shape,
Land and water were taking form.
A stirring rod divided the land,
Water was separated with a dipper.
Greening, the young grass grew.
This was in the time,
When on the crowns of trees,
Forty birds chirped,
When young nightingales sang
Above the green grass.
It was springtime!

-2-

With seventy mountain passes
The blue mountain stands.
At the foot of the blue mountain
With the seventy passes, surging
The blue sea flows!
On the shore of the blue sea
Uncountable livestock grazes,
A multitudinous people lives.
In the midst of that *ulus*-village,
Stands a golden palace.
At the golden palace,
At the golden hitching post,
Which no horse can uproot,
Stands a three-ears blue-grey horse,

The best of horses.
Inside the golden palace,
Lived Kёk Kan,
He who filled the white world at his birth.
Kёk Kan's wife, Kёk Torgu,
Bustling, moves the table,
Effortless, sets out food,
Repeating:
– *Eze,* Kёk Kan, my husband, sit down,
Try this meal!
About the time when they had their fill of food,
The earth's surface swayed,
The bottom of the earth shuddered.
Throwing open the hinged window, they saw:
A dark chestnut horse descending,
The mountain ridge, where no strange horse treads.

-3-
As big as a block of mountain, the *alyp*[3] sits
On a dark chestnut horse.
With the thunder of a hundred horses, his horse gallops,
With the cry of a hundred *bogatyrs*, the *alyp* yells:
– Is the three-eared blue-gray horse at the hitching post?
Is Kёk Kan at home?
If you are an *alyp*, we will duel,
If you are a fighter, we will battle!
Come out here! – he calls.
Seeing this, hearing this, Kёk Kan
Leapt up from the golden table:
– *Eze*, my wife Kёk Torgu, – he said, –
Be in good health.
The best of the *alyps* entered, – he said –
Arriving on horseback
On the best dark chestnut horse.

Will my pure strength suffice or will it not?
That *alyp* called me out,
You heard so yourself, – and so saying,
He bowed and bade them farewell,
He set out and donned
The nine-layered golden hauberk.
Buttoning the nine buttons,
He walked out of the golden palace.

-4-

Leaving the golden palace
He looked closely:
The descendant of *alyps*, driving his horse
Downward along the slope!
Kёk Kan rode forward to meet him,
And they met at the center of the white steppe.
The *alyps'* descendant leapt from his horse,
And grabbed Kёk Kan by his breast.
Grasping him thusly,
Together they circled and began to fight:
An impenetrable pitch black
Fog fell.
Birds left their nests.
Animals abandoned their offspring.
When they collided with the blue mountain,
The black cliff of the blue mountain
Rained a *kurumnik* of stones down upon them.
As they battled, they crossed
The blue sea,
Turning it to mud:
Thusly they battled.
They battled and battled:
They guess
That summer had come

By the heat, sun beating down on their shoulders.

They learn

That winter had arrived

By the snow covering their heads and shoulders.

Nine days passed.

After nine days,

The surefooted Kёk Kan,

Blundered.

The unerring Kёk Kan,

Erred.

Then Kёk Kan asked the *bogatyr's* descendant:

You came to my land

To steal my livestock,

To steal my people, you came.

What sort of *alyp* will you be?

What harm did I ever do you? – the other asked.

What sort of *alyp* will I be?

I came from the sixty worlds.

Master of the black mountain and

Sixty mountain passes,

I am Kara Kaia on the dark chestnut horse.

Eze, Kёk Kan, – he said, –

When I've destroyed your pure soul

I will steal your white livestock

All the same, – he said.

Then he began to shake

Kёk Kan like a sack;

He began to twist him, like a strap.

The never tearful Kёk Kan

Began to cry.

Kёk Kan, sobbing, says:

– *Eze*, my wife Kёk Torgu,

Standing before me, there will be no one to intercede.

Covering the rear,

There will be no one to support me, – he said. –
It is time for me to leave this white world, –
And so saying, he cries.

-5-

During this time when he was crying,
The earth's surface swayed,
The bottom of the *chegen*-earth shook.
Then they saw:
A newborn boy was descending
Wearing a blue robe, closed with three buttons,
On the mountain ridge,
Where strange horses do not tread.
Having descended, he said:
– Look!
In order to reach the pure soul of Këk Kan
For whom there is no one to intercede,
This descendant of the *alyps* has come, – he said. –
Having come down,
I will give him one of my arrows[4], – and so saying,
He ran down.
Having reached the bottom, he grasped Këk Kan
And so threw him out into the white steppe that
He went head over heels.
He grasped the *alyps'* descendant by the chest,
And prevented him from stepping here, there,
And having gathered him into a heap from the black earth,
He began to raise him to the forty heavens.
When he raised him up to the forty heavens,
The child said:
– *Eze*, Kara Kaia, you *alyp*,
Is there anyone stronger than you, *alyp*,
On this white earth? – he said.
Hearing this, Kara Kaia:

May your name be damned,
Këk Olak! – he said. –
I am losing
The strength of the earth, the strength of the heavens.
Your strength surpasses
Me, a descendant of *alyps*, – he said. –
From here,
Beyond the boundaries of the forty lands,
Resides Kara Kan Mergen,
Master of the black mountain
With nine mountain passes.
Go to his land.
Will they not break apart
Your smoothly grown backbone? – he said.
Thank you, Kara Kaia! – said Këk Olak
And untangling his mouth, he barked:
I have set forth to break up
The backbone of the *alyps'* descendant into nine pieces!

-6-

Then Këk Olak approached Këk Kan,
Turning to him, he said:
– *Eze*, Këk Kan,
Now you are like a father to me, Këk Kan!
The single creator,
Having turned me into a golden egg, threw me:
"There is no one to stand and intercede
For Këk Kan!
Having descended, save his pure soul!" –
So commanding, he threw, – Këk Olak says. –
He says. – The single creator sent
Me thusly, having made me. –
Eze, Këk Kan, having become my father,
Now, – said Këk Olak, – from here,

The immortal, undying
Kara Kan Mergen is
Beyond the borders of the forty lands.
He related, – I will go to the land of the
Immortal-undying Kara Kan Mergen.
Many *alyps* have appeared
On this white earth,
However, having gashes in their heads, I will fix it.
– *Pai-pai*, boy in the blue coat,
Buttoned with three buttons,
I ask you to intercede on my behalf!
Where are you going?
Stop by, partake of a meal, –
Invited Kёk Kan.
– No, Kёk Kan, refused Kan Olak, –
I will go there, where you had planned to go, –
So saying, the boy turned away,
And set off at a run,
Where did he go? Where did he arrive?!

-7-

I have stayed with the child![5]
As he was on foot, the boy
Set off at a run, hiking up his robes.
He ran, looking ahead!
I can say it quickly,
He has a long way to travel![6]
Then he sees:
The peak of the black mountain
With forth mountain passes is visible!
When the peak of the mountain
With forty passes became visible,
He sank into the embrace of the mountain's saddle,
Descending along the smooth ridge

From the foot of the black mountain.
He looked carefully about:
The livestock was settled,
The people were living after all.
The three-eared dark chestnut horse stood
At the golden hitching post
That no horse can uproot
Outside the golden palace.
Seeing this, Këk Olak,
Galloped like a hundred horses,
Calling out like a hundred horses:
Is the three-eared dark chestnut horse
Tied up? –
Is Kara Kan Mergen at home?
If you are an *alyp*, we will duel,
If you are a fighter, we will battle!
Come out here! – challenged Këk Olak.
Then he sees:
The hinged doors fly open.
An *alyp* the size of a black mountain steps
Out of the golden palace.
Coming out, the descendant of the *alyps* said:
– *Pai-pai*, *alyps* were wary and have not
Entered into my land in the past, – he said. –
Look at that, the *alyp* entered defiantly.
Stepping off the golden porch,
Kara Kan Mergen walked forward to meet him.
With a shout, this Këk Olak continued down toward him
– *Eze*, Këk Olak, in the blue robe,
Closed with three buttons, it is you.
Is the white world is so unpleasant to you,
That you come to battle with me!
I will break
Your smoothly grown backbone into pieces!

Only a piece of meat will remain of you,
Only a tiny bowl of blood will remain! –
Muttering so to himself, he approached,
And grasped Kёk Olak by the chest.
Kёk Olak also grabbed
Kara Kan Mergen by the chest.
They fought and turned with all their strength
Such that a black fog fell
Over this land.
As they circled, holding each other by the chest,
Kёk Olak asked:
– *Eze*, Kara Kan Mergen,
Are there *alyps*
Stronger than you in the white world?
Hearing this, Kara Kan Mergen replied:
– *Pai-pai*, Kёk Olak,
Dressed in a blue robe
Held together with three buttons,
Are you asking me, Kan Mergen,
Who believes himself stronger?
After all, there are *alyps* stronger than I.
From here, beyond the thirty worlds,
Beyond the thirty khanates,
Is Lower Kan Mergen
Living together with High Kan Mergen, – he replied. –
No *alyp* from anywhere in the white world
Goes into their lands to issue a challenge!
– If that's the case, Kara Kan Mergen,
Thank you very much! – acknowledged Kёk Olak.
He did not allow Kara Kan Mergen to move about,
But crumpling him, he lifted him off the black earth,
Raising him to the forty heavens.
Seeing this, feeling this,
Kara Kan Mergen rose with a cry:

– Damn you,
Kёk Olak in the blue robe,
Fastened with three buttons.
He said, – I am rising up, having lost
The strength of the earth, the strength of the heavens!
If you do, honestly,
Possess unusual strength, Kёk Olak,
When you travel to the land of
The Lower Kan Mergen
And the High Kan Mergen,
They will break
Your smooth backbone into pieces! – calling out,
He ascended.
Kёk Olak, having twisted him,
Threw Kara Kan Mergen against
A black stone
That looked larger than a cow:
Kara Kan Mergen's backbone
Broke apart into nine pieces.
Having conquered his pure soul,
The boy in the blue robe
Fastened with three buttons,
Turned away,
From the field of battle, bouncing, and ran off:
Who knows where,
He ran.

-8-
He ran and ran;
Pulling his robe to the side, he runs.
Then he sees:
The peak of the grey mountain
With eighty mountain passes
Emerging as it touches the heavens.

He sank into the embrace of the mountain's saddle,
Descending along the smooth ridge
To the foot of the grey mountain
With the eighty passes.
And saw:
The white livestock was grazing,
The numerous people lives.
Looking around, he saw:
A golden palace is there.
The tip of the golden palace
Peeked through the black mountain
With the eighty passes,
Where it stands.
Next he sees:
A short grey horse
Was standing alongside a tall grey horse
At the golden hitching post
No horse can uproot
Near the golden palace.
They stood
Having punched through three layers
Of the black earth.

-9-
Seeing this, Kёk Olak,
Ran with the thunder of a hundred horses,
Called out with the cry of a hundred *alyps*:
– Older-Younger
Dark chestnut horses at the hitching post, –
Lower Kan Mergen
And High Kan Mergen,
If you are *alyps*, then to duel,
If you are fighters, then come out to battle! –
He called out.

Then he sees:
The doors of the golden palace flew open,
And two *alyps* stepped out of the golden palace.
Angered, they said:
– Look, High Kan Mergen, my older brother,
An *alyp* has come into our land
To challenge us, – said Lower Kan Mergen. –
Usually *alyps* steer wide of our land.
And now an *alyp* has come straight in
With a challenge!
Let us go and
Break the smooth backbone of this
Kĕk Olak into pieces! – so saying,
The two bogatyrs stepped off the golden porch.
When Kĕk Olak ran forward to meet them,
They too walked forward.
Meeting in the white steppe,
Lower Kan Mergen approached,
Grabbing Kĕk Olak by the broad chest:
– If you find the white world unpleasant,
I will send you out of the white world.
A rabbit landing in our arms
No longer runs about
The white world, – so saying,
He grasped Kĕk Olak by the chest.
They began to battle:
An impenetrable pitch black
Fog fell.
Three days they fought.
After three days Kĕk Olak asked:
– *Eze*, Lower Kan Mergen,
Are there *alyps* stronger than you
In the white world?
– *Pai-pai*, Kĕk Olak, – he answered, –

You ask as if
You had already conquered our souls.
Are there *alyps* stronger than us? – he repeated. –
Down below, beyond sixty layers of earth,
Kara Turtus lives together with Kara Kazan,
When you conquer our souls,
Go down to them, – he said.
– Thank you very much,
Lower Kan Mergen, – and so saying, Kёk Olak
Tore him away from the black earth,
And began to lift him
To the forty heavens.
When he had lifted him to the forty heavens,
Lower Kan Mergen,
Crying, is ascending.
– *Eze*, High Kan Mergen, my brother,
This is Kёk Olak who lost his name!
Together he raises, – he says
The strength of the earth, strength of heaven.
Kёk Olak twisted Lower Kan Mergen.
There was a black stone.
Aiming at the black stone
Larger than a cow, he threw him:
Shattering his backbone
In nine places, he released him.
Go, High Kan Mergen, – he said.
High Kan Mergen ran forward:
– Look, here nearby, – he said, –
I allow you to destroy
The pure soul of Lower Kan Mergen.
But wait, Kёk Olak,
I will break your smoothly grown body
Into pieces, – so said High Kan Mergen.
Grasping each other by the broad chest,

They circled each other for three days.

After three days:

– *Eze*, older brother Kan Mergen, – said Kёk Olak, –

Your younger brother Kan Mergen told me,

That there are *alyps* stronger than you!, – he said.

– If, truth be told, you are so strong, – he replied, –

Go down to the sixtieth layer of earth.

Go into the arms of Kara Turtus and Kara Kazan,

Only a piece of meat will remain from you

Only a bowl of blood will remain! – he shouted.

And Kёk Olak began to lift

The elder Kan Mergen

From the black earth, crushing and gathering him,

To the forty heavens.

When he lifted him to the forty heavens,

The brother, crying, ascended.

– You, having lost your name, Kёk Olak!

Together with the strength of earth and heavens,

I am ascending, – mourned High Kan Mergen.

Kёk Olak turned the *bogatyr*,

And there was a white stone,

Larger than a cow in size.

Aiming at the stone, he tossed him:

Breaking his backbone in nine places,

And having shattered him, released him.

-10-

Turning away, Kёk Olak set off at a run.

No one knew where he was headed.

He ran to the entrance-*tyundyuk*[7] of the Earth.

Having reached the entrance-*tyundyuk* of the Earth,

– Here is the place where they descend

Into the Underworld! – so saying, –

He set out immediately

At a run into the Underworld.
Kёk Olak went down and down:
Past the borders
Of the sixty layers of the Earth he went down.
Then he sees:
Beyond the sixty layers of the Earth
The black Mount *Non*
With sixty mountain passes
Arranged in a circle.
Having reached the foot of the black Mount *Non*,
Then he sees:
A black palace with seventy corners.

-11-
He ran up to the black palace with seventy corners,
He ran up to the black building,
And with a cry, he went in:
– *Eze*, Kara Turtus and Kara Kazan,
Do you live here?
If you are *alyps* we will duel,
Come here, – he cried out.
Running forward, he sees:
The hinged doors opened wide,
Two *alyps*, like black mountains,
Stepping out, they look about, surprised:
– Look, Kara Kazan-brother, – said one of the *bogatyrs*, –
An *alyp* can issue a challenge
Even in our land!
He did not fear us.
There have not been *alyps*
From the world of the sun, – they said, –
In our black land of the *aina*-devil
There have not been such *alyps*.
We will break his smooth tall body

Into pieces! – so saying,
The brothers stepped down from the iron porch,
And set out to meet Këk Olak.
Running forward, Këk Olak and Kara Turtus
Grasped each other by their broad chests,
And thus they whirled about:
An impenetrable pitch
Black fog fell.
They battled for up to six days.
After six days:
The sure-footed Kara Turtus
Began to stumble,
The agile Kara Turtus
Began to trip.
The boy in the blue robe,
Fastened with three buttons, asked:
– *Eze*, Kara Turtus,
Are there *alyps*
In the white world
In the land of the black *aina*-devils
That are stronger than you?
– You who have lost your name, Këk Olak, – answered Kara
    Turtus. –
From here, under the ninetieth layer of the Earth lives
Kara Shoyun is here,
The immortal, undying,
And strength unknowing *alyp*, – he said.
So, if you are so strong,
Go down there, – said Kara Turtus. –
When you land in the clutches of Kara Shoyun,
The immortal will die,
The undying will perish, –
And thus shouting, he ascended.
When he had raised Kara Turtus

To the ninth heaven above the Earth,
Having spun him about, he threw him
Onto a black stone larger than a cow:
He shattered his backbone in nine places.
From there Kёk Olak turned,
And ran off into the deepest depths,
Under the ninetieth layer of the Earth.

-12-

Having set off,
He began to descend under ninety layers of earth.
He went down and down:
And then he sees:
He descended down ninety layers of the Earth.
It was a dark, twilight land!
Under the ninety layers of earth,
There appeared
A black mountain with ninety mountain passes
Filling the entire earth!
He sank into the embrace of the mountain's saddle,
Descending to the foot of the black mountain,
Along the smooth ridge.
Then he sees:
The black building with ninety corners stood there.
An iron hitching post stood
Outside the black building with ninety corners.
A dark bay horse stands
At the iron hitching post.
The forty-sazhen[8] bay horse stands.
He had stomped through
This black earth to the sixth layer!
Seeing this, Kёk Olak,
Ran with the thunder of a hundred horses,
Calling with shouts of a hundred *alyps*:

– Was the forty-*sazhen* dark bay horse
Tied at the hitching post?
Was the immortal undying
Kara Shoyun inside the black building?
If there is an *alyp* then come forth to duel,
If there is a fine fellow, then come forth to battle! – he calls.
Then he sees:
The hinged doors of the black building opened,
The *alyp*'s descendant came out.
He could only go out the door sideways!
The *alyp* walked out like a black mountain,
Angered, he says:
– Great woe,
Great surprise!
An *alyp* has come to my land with a challenge!
There have been no *alyps*
In either the Upper world of the sun or in the Lower world,
That did not fear me.
Now that a strong *alyp* has come,
I will break his smoothly-grown body
Into pieces! – so saying,
He stepped off the iron porch.
They walked toward each other.
This Këk Olak also ran upward.
Meeting,
They grasped each other by the chest and circled about:
This Earth is no longer earth,
This river is no longer a river!
They battled for nine days.
After nine days:
The surefooted Kara Shoyun,
Began to stumble, and he said:
– *Pai-pai*, it is you who has lost your name,
Këk Olak in the blue robe,

Fastened with three buttons!
You were born an *alyp*
You have so exhausted me, Kara Shoyun,
That I have begun to stumble!
– *Eze*, Kara Shoyun, – answered Këk Olak, –
Tell me,
Are there *alyps* stronger than you
On the white earth
In the land of black *aina*-devils? – he asked.
Hearing this, Kara Shoyun said:
Këk Olak who lost his name, –
If you, truly, are so strong, – he said, –
There is an *alyp* stronger than me,
Kuba Salgyn of the forty wives.
Kuba Salgyn with the light chestnut horse,
He has a true wife from the Upper world!
The daughter of Kyun Kan from the bright world, – he said, –
Living under the sun, he took her, and she lives,
This is his first, true wife!
His second true wife, – he said, –
Is the daughter of Ay Kan, Ay Këk, and he took her to wife,
And she lives under forty layers of earth.
If you are so strong,
Make your way to Kuba Salgyn, – he said. –
Kuba Salgyn
Will put you in one hand,
And the other will strike you so hard,
That your soul will tumble out! – he said.
– Thank you, Kara Shoyun! – Këk Olak acknowledged.
And crumpling him and scooping him from the black earth,
He lifted him to the nine layers of the heavens,
And turning, so struck him
That Kara Shoyun was driven
Into the black earth to his waist!

So departed the pure soul of Kara Shoyun in flight.

-13-

Turning away from there,

He ran toward the Upper world.

Above

He ran in the direction of the world of the sun.

From there, he ran down

Under forty layers under the earth.

Then he sees:

Ahead, stood a white mountain

With forty mountain passes.

He sank into the embrace of the mountain's saddle,

Descending to the foot of the black mountain,

Along the smooth ridge.

Then he sees:

White livestock is grazing,

The numerous people lives.

The livestock of the world of the sun,

The people of the world of the sun lived.

Then he sees:

A flaxen-maned chestnut horse stands

At the golden hitching post.

There were no more horses.

Approaching the golden hitching post,

Then he sees:

– Great woe, – he said, –

There stands a horse from the world of the sun!

People of the world of the sun,

Livestock of the world of the sun stand!

He went into the golden palace.

Opening the doors, he made greeting.

Crossing the threshold, he bowed.

He looks:

An old man sits
At the golden table.
He sits with his wife.
A girl sat off to the side from them.
When this Kёk Olak, having opened the doors, made greeting,
Crossing the threshold, bowing,
The girl and the woman
Glanced at him in surprise,
Greeted and bowed in return.
– *Alyps* come to our land as well.
Eze, it is you, Kёk Olak in the blue robe,
Fastened with three buttons!
Why have you come to us? –
Asked the old man.
– *Eze*, – Kёk Olak greeted, –
Are you, Ay Kan, he who lives
Beyond the forty layers of the Earth?
– I am Ay Kan! – the old man replied.
– *Pai-pai*, Ay Kan, – said Kёk Olak, –
I see
Your white livestock from the world of the sun,
Your numerous people –
People of the world of the sun, – he said.
The horse that you ride, –
Is the best of all horses, this flaxen chestnut horse.
What sort of *alyp* will you be?
Why are you the *alyp* living here? –
Asked Kёk Olak curiously.
– *Eze*, Kёk Olak, – answered Ay Kan, –
By the single creator, damn him, I
Was sent down here.
Now I live under forty layers of earth.
I am an *alyp* from the land of the sun, – he said. –
I, Ay Kan,

Used to live under the golden mountain
With sixty mountain passes,
Which stood under the sun,
Stood under the moon, – he said.
– *Eze,* Ay Kan, – said Këk Olak, –
Kuba Salgyn with the light chestnut horse,
Who is he to you?
– He is my son-in-law! – he replied.
– Where is your son-in-law?
– Where can he be? – he said. –
He lives on the Earth under the sun.
Well, his true wife lives
At the foot of the golden mountain
With sixty passes.
He lives there.
That Kyun Kan –
He is my older brother.
I am his younger brother,
Ay Kan, I will be, – he said. –
Now he lives in the land of Kyun Kan!
He lives for forty days,
When he descends to this place, with my daughter.
This is my daughter,
Well, Ay Aryg, daughter, – he said, –
He lives here with her for forty days, and then ascends.
Reaching the land of Kyun Kan,
Brother, he goes in.
There with the daughter of my brother Kyun Kan,
He lives with the girl Kyun Aryg
For forty days, – he says. –
As he has forty wives,
He spends one night with each wife.
And thus he lives!
Why do you seek him? – asked Ay Kan.

– Why do I seek him? – repeated Kёk Olak, –
I want to take the measure of his pure strength.
– *Pai-pai*, Kёk Olak, – he said, –
You are not the *alyp* to battle
With this immortal and undying
Kuba Salgyn, my son-in-law.
For Kuba Salgyn, immortal, undying,
Is my son-in-law, – he said. –
There are no *alyps* in the Upper world
Or in the world of the black *aina*-devils,
Who do not fear him, who have not been vexed by him.
– *Che*[9], Ay Kan, – he said, –
Thank you!
I have said all I wanted to say!
And then they seated him at the golden table,
And plied him with food.
– *Che*, Ay Kan, said Kёk Olak, –
Thank you.
He sat for six days,
He ate and ate.
Since I was born,
I have not tried food.
Now I will ascend
To the land of Kyun Kan, – he said.
He bade them farewell and bowed,
Leaving the golden palace,
And leapt from the golden porch such that
He landed up to his knees
In the black earth!
When the boy ran from there,
The whole earth swayed!

-14-

When he ran through Ay Kan's land,

He sees: approaching him the three-eared
Blue-grey horse of Kĕk Kan at a gallop.
Then he sees:
A nine-layered golden hauberk was thrown
Sideways
Across the golden saddle
Of the three-eared blue-grey horse of Kĕk Kan.
An urgent note was written
On the pommel of the golden saddle:
"Boy in the blue robe,
Fastened with three buttons,
You went under the earth.
I, the sole creator who gave you a name,
Banish you! – it was written thus. –
Henceforth from today, you, the son of Kĕk Kan
Riding on the three-eared blue-grey horse
Will be named Kĕk Torchuk!" –
Thus was written.
Seeing this, Kĕk Olak,
And grasping the nine-layered
Golden hauberk, he began to don it.
Donning the nine-layered
Golden hauberk, he said:
– *Eze*, blue-grey horse,
How did you come to meet me? – he said.
– It was foreordained
By the sole creator-*chaiachy*! – answered the horse. –
Having received the name Kĕk Torchuk,
You became a son of Kĕk Kan,
With a three-eared
Blue-grey horse from Kĕk Kan!
This was foreordained by the sole creator.
– Fine, blue-grey horse, – agreed Kĕk Torchuk.
And he clung to the blue-grey horse like a bat,

Turning the horse, he drove it further.

-15-

He rode out from under the earth to the white world,
And then he rode through the white world.
As he rode, he sees:
Ahead, a golden mountain
With sixty mountain passes appearing.
He sank into the embrace of the mountain's saddle,
Descending to the foot of the black mountain,
Along the smooth ridge,
He looked about attentively:
The white livestock were scattered,
The numerous people were settled.
Among the numerous people
Stands a golden palace.
At the golden palace he sees:
A flaxen-maned chestnut horse stands.
Alongside the flaxen-maned
Chestnut horse
Stands a light chestnut horse.
Having seen this,
He gallops with the thunder of a hundred horses,
And cries with the voices of a hundred *alyps*:
– The light chestnut horse
Stands at the golden mountain
Outside the golden palace.
Kuba Salgyn is inside Kyun Kan's palace!
Come out here,
If you are an *alyp*, then to duel,
If you are a fine fellow, then to battle, come out! –
So he cried out.
Then he sees:
The hinged doors of the golden palace flew open,

And the *alyp*'s descendant comes out:
The entire steppe was blinded
By the nine-layered golden hauberk
Made with fish scales.
There he says:
– *Pai-pai*, Kĕk Olak
In the blue robe
Fastened with three buttons, – he said. –
Now you have received the name Kĕk Torchuk.
Why have you come to our land
With a challenge? – so says Kuba Salgyn.
He stepped down from the golden porch.
And set out on the white steppe.
The other *alyp* drove his blue-grey horse forward to meet him.
When they met,
He leapt from the horse,
And grasped Kuba Salgyn by the chest!
When he leapt from the blue-grey horse,
And grasped Kuba Salgyn by the chest –
Kuba Salgyn said:
– *Pai-pai*, Kĕk Torchuk, – he said, –
Why do you grasp me by the chest?
Having become brothers,
We will live together! – he said. –
The sole creator put you
In a golden egg, – he said, –
In order that you save Kĕk Kan.[10]
The sole creator also
Threw me in the form of a golden egg.
And I rolled off, – he said, –
To the middle of the earth
To the foot of the golden mountain.
Here my true wife,
Kyun Aryg, daughter of Kyun Kan,

And my second true wife –
Daughter of Ay Kan, – he said, –
Lives beyond the forty layers of earth.
Her name is Ay Aryg.
Let us live together,
Now that we are brothers.
Why do you seize hold of me?
– *Eze*, Kuba Salgyn, – answered Kёk Torchuk, –
There is only one khan in the white world,
Only one *piy*-leader can exist, – and so saying,
When a bad dog bites,
When a rabid cow began to butt its horns.
Kuba Salgyn begged him for nine days:
– *Eze*, Kёk Torchuk, – he persuaded, –
Let us live together, as brothers!
For there are no more
Alyps that we must fear
In the white world.
We shall live together
Having become brothers.
– No, Kuba Salgyn, – he replied, –
I ascended
In order to capture your pure soul!
And I will conquer your pure soul.
Hearing this, Kuba Salgyn said:
– *Che*, Kёk Torchuk, – he said, –
I will not raise my fists to you.
I will not battle with you.
You are my brother, – he said. –
If you want to conquer my soul,
Then take my pure soul,
I will rise up myself!
You do not have enough pure strength
To lift me

To the forty heavens, to beat me.
I will go up myself, – he said.
And after forty days
Kuba Salgyn began to climb by himself
To the forty heavens.
Twisting him, Kёk Torchuk
So struck him –
That he was buried to his waist in the black earth,
And conquered his pure soul!
He ran from there,
To the blue-grey horse
And clung to him like a bat.
Turning away
He clung to the blue-grey horse
Like a bat,
Then he sees:
Kyun Aryg running out of the golden palace,
Where she fell upon Kuba Salgyn,
Disconsolately beginning to sob:
– *Eze*, dear Kuba Salgyn,
I married you for love, – she said. –
For you are not the sort of *alyp*
That can be conquered?
Why did you rise up yourself,
You should have let yourself be beaten! – she sobbed.

-16-
Seeing this, Kёk Torchuk
So raked the sides of
The three-eared blue-grey horse,
That it is unknowable where he landed.
As he galloped, he said:
– *Eze*, three-eared blue-grey horse,
Along the way we will visit

The girl that I will marry.
She is at the far end of this land,
She lives at the end of this distant land, – he said. –
Ak Kan is here, – he said, –
Whose birth filled with white world.
Ak Kan, whose birth filled
The white world,
Has a daughter, Ala Manak.
I will take this girl, – and so saying,
He pressed his horse onward.
He rode and rode:
His father's land passed out of memory,
His mother's land passed out of the spirit.[11]
No one knows what land he traverses.
I say this quickly, *eze*,
But his journey is slow![12]
He rode and he rode:
At the very end of the land,
At the edge of the land, he began to ascend.
Then he sees:
Ahead, growing up to the sky,
A white mountain appeared
With seventy passes.
He sank into the embrace of the mountain's saddle,
Descending along the smooth ridge
To the foot of the white mountain
With seventy passes.
Then he sees:
Many *alyps* had gathered
In this land!
The *alyps* of the white world,
Sat, having squashed the white *taskyl*-mountain.
The black *aina*-devils, sat
Having flattened the black *taskyl*

Steam rose from the pot
Reaching up to the forty heavens.
Meat with forty ears simmered
In black kettles
Forty *chaizan*-shepherds approach,
And spill out the meat from the pot.
Seven *chaizans* walk
Around the copper kettle with seven ears
And pour out the meat.
When he had descended, he saw:
The best of horses were hitched
To the golden hitching post!
Among the horses, a wonderful
Flaxen-maned
Light chestnut horse was tied.
The roots of grass blackened by flame
Out of his two burning eyes.
A dark chestnut horse
Stood alongside.
The horse stood
Having stomped through six layers of earth.
Alongside the dark chestnut horse
Stood a dark brown horse
With a velvety coat.
The horse stood
Having stomped through six layers of earth.
Seeing this, Kĕk Torchuk thinks:
"*Adanmada*, the best of horses are here!
What sorts of *alyps*
Ride upon them?"

-17-
Kĕk Torchuk leapt
From the three-eared blue-grey horse.

Opening the door, he walked
Into the golden palace and gave greeting.
He bowed upon crossing the threshold:
All the *alyps*
Welcomed him with one voice!
– *Adanmada*, – they said, –
The blue-grey horse, the best of all horses, has arrived at a gallop!
– *Adanmada*, the best of *alyps*
The *alyp* has come! – they said,
Three *alyps*
Leapt up from the table:
– We arrived long ago,
The body has gone numb, – so saying, –
They gave up their places.
Kёk Torchuk walked forward,
And sat in the place of those three *alyps*.
Sitting at the golden table, he began to look about:
The best of the best *alyps* sat here!
One *alyp*
Was dressed in a nine-layered golden hauberk:
A single one of his eyes
Was like a roiling white sea.
The other eye
Was like a roaring black sea!
– *Eze*, this unusual *bogatyr*,
Is the best of *alyps*!
What kind of *alyp* will you be? – asked Kёk Torchuk?
What kind of *alyp* will I be? – he said, –
I am Altyn Shur,
Riding on a flaxen-maned light chestnut horse.
Sitting alongside him, a different descendant of an *alyp* sat,
He was like a mountain, he was!
– And you, what sort of *alyp* will you be? – he asked.
– What kind of *alyp* will I be?

I am Kara Salgyn, riding
On a dark chestnut horse, – he said.
An *alyp* sat alongside him,
Big, like a mountain!
What kind of *alyp* will you be? – asked Kёk Torchuk?
What kind of *alyp* will I be?
I will be Kyuren Kylysh, riding
On a dark brown horse
With a velvety mane, – he said.
As they sat, conversing:
A descendant of the *alyps*, dressed in a golden hauberk,
Walked in, carrying a white cask under his arms.
Approaching, he filled the golden goblet
Which sixty *alyps* cannot drain
With wine:
– *Eze*, descendant of an *alyp*, – he said, –
You came from afar.
And since you came from afar,
Your mouth has gone numb from thirst, – he said, –
When you drink the wine of the great khan,
Your mouth-tongue will speak more easily,
And then I will question you about your name-clan!
Seeing this, Kёk Torchuk
Lifted the golden goblet
With his right hand
And drank it in one gulp!
– What kind of *alyp* are you, –
Asked the descendant of the *alyps*, dressed in a golden hauberk, –
You who arrived on the best of horses,
A three-eared blue-gray horse?
– What sort of *alyp* am I? – answered Kёk Torchuk. –
I am Kёk Torchuk,
Son of Kёk Kan,
Master of the blue mountain

With seventy passes,
And I ride on a three-eared blue-grey horse!
– I'll give you that! – he said. –
We have not heard of such an *alyp.*
As they sat and ate,
Kёk Torchuk inquired:
– *Eze*, Ak Kan will give me
His daughter Ala Manak in marriage:
He wishes to organize a contest
Or, he will give her to the *alyps*
To cut her into pieces? – he asked. –
Why is this great contest unacceptable?
The he sees:
The nine doors of the rooms opened widely,
And coming in, the descendant of the *alyps* proclaimed:
– Let those with ears hear! –
Let those with eyes see! – he said. –
I will put on a great contest
For my daughter Ala Manak, – so he said. –
Let those with eyes see!
Let those with ears hear!
I will give away my daughter
To the *alyp* of those of you gathered here
Whose horse has fast legs! – he said. –
I will give my daughter
To the *alyp* of those gathered here
Who can dump everyone into a single hole,
I proclaim, I give glory! – so he said.
Hearing this, the *alyps* leapt up,
And they began to leave
The golden palace, jostling each other.

-18-
After they had left:

Four *alyps* remained
After all the *alyps* had left.
Kёk Torchuk then sees:
Of the remaining *alyps*
Altyn Shur, removed the saddle
From his flaxen-maned light chestnut horse,
As if making a heap.
Kara Salgyn, removed the saddle
From his dark chestnut horse,
As if making a heap.
Kyuren Kylysh, removed the saddle
From his dark brown horse,
As if making a heap.
Having kept their four horses nearby, they
Set them free:
Where did the horses run, what place did they reach?
Turning about, the men
Went into the golden palace.
– Let the horses travel
The white world nine times! – said the *alyps*,
They sat at the golden table
And began to partake of food.
They sat and they sat,
They sat for nine days.
After nine days
From the height of forty heavens
The golden cuckoo began to sing:
– *Alyps*, what are you doing
Sitting there in the golden palace?
The horses are already returning! – the bird cuckooed.
Hearing this, the *alyps*
Jostled each other
As they began to leave the golden palace.
These four

Came out after all the other *alyps*.
Then Kёk Torchuk sees:
A white woven thread stretched
Across the peak of the white *taskyl* mountain.
They ascended to the peak of the white *taskyl* mountain.
Having reached the peak of the white *taskyl* mountain,
They looked about:
Dust from the black earth
Rose up to the heavens.
Kёk Torchuk looked about and thought,
That a blue butterfly was flying
In the black fog,
And the three-eared blue-grey horse ran out!
Trailing six sazhens behind
The three-eared blue-grey horse,
The flaxen-maned light chestnut horse
And the dark brown horse
Galloped neck and neck!
Seeing this, the descendants of the *alyps*
Cried out!
The best of the horses
Ran up to the foot of the white *taskyl* mountain.
Without touching the white thread with his front feet,
Nor his hind feet
The three-eared blue-grey horse,
Leapt over the white thread.

-19-
Seeing this, Kёk Torchuk yelled out:
– The contest of the horses is mine!
Let the person who desired to take away my girl,
Come to me! – he shouted.
Then Kёk Torchuk sees:
Altyn Shur, owner of the flaxen-maned

Slight chestnut horse,
Rolls up his sleeves to his elbows
And sets forth, throwing open his robe!
Approaching, Altyn Shur said:
– Wait, Kёk Torchuk,
The horse of one *alyp*
Turned out to have faster legs.
One *alyp*
Turned out to have more strength, – he said. –
I would close my chokecherry eyes
I would lay down my head, my egg,
Before I would give you up
Ak Kan's daughter, Ala Manak to you, – so saying Altyn Shur,
Grasped Kёk Torchuk by the broad chest.
Then, together they grappled,
And how they spun around:
An impenetrable pitch
Black fog fell!
They fought for almost six years.
After six years
Kёk Torchuk surged like a whirlwind,
Flew, like the wind.
When he began to tackle Altyn Shur
With a yell,
He set him down on hands and knees,
– Wait, Altyn Shur, – Kёk Torchuk began to ask, –
You are the best *alyp*.
Surely you have enough girls in this white world,
That you do not need to come after my betrothed? – he asked. –
If you do not require the white world,
I will acquire your pure soul, – and so saying,
He drove him up the slope
And down the slope.
Dragging him on his left side, his right side,

He began to lift him from the black earth.
Lifting him to the forty heavens,
He twisted him and tossed him so that –
The earth created by the *Kudai*-creator
Swayed throughout.
He was driven into the ground
Up to his waist.
Opening his two eyes wide,
His pure soul leapt out.
Then he sees:
Kara Salgyn rolled his sleeves to his elbows,
Throwing open
The two panels of his robe!
– Wait, Kёk Torchuk, – he said, –
Having taken Altyn Shur's pure soul,
You rejoiced greatly
That you are taking the girl Ala Manak away.
I will break into pieces
Your graceful spine, – so saying, he went forward.
Grasping both of the *alyps* by their broad chests.
Together they grappled,
Circling:
An impenetrable pitch
Black fog fell everywhere!
Again they fight
For almost six years.
After six years
Kёk Torchuk surged like a whirlwind
Flew like the wind.
And put Kara Salgyn down on hands and knees:
– Wait, Kara Salgyn, – he said, –
If you have come for my Ala Manak,
Not having found a different girl in the white world.
I will break your graceful spine

Into pieces, – so saying Kёk Torchuk,
He began to drive him up the slope
He began to drive him down the slope.
He raised him up to the forty heavens
And twisting him, he so cast him down
The earth created by the *Kudai*-creator
Swayed like a cradle.
Then Kёk Torchuk sees:
He drove Kara Salgyn into the earth
Up to his waist.
The other raised his eyes to the forty heavens,
And his pure soul leapt out.
Then Kёk Torchuk sees:
Kyuren Kylysh set out, throwing open
The two panels of his robe
And rolling his sleeves up to his elbows!
– Wait, Kёk Torchuk, – he said, –
Do not think,
That you are the only one in this white world.
Then he approached, and grasped him by the broad chest.
The two *alyps* circled together:
Tossing each other as animals toss their children.
As birds leave their nests.
They again fought for almost six years.
After six years
Kёk Torchuk surged like a whirlwind,
Flew like the wind.
Tore Kyuren Kylysh away from the black earth!
Lifted him to the forty heavens,
And twisting him, he so cast him down
That the black earth
Swayed throughout, like a black cradle.
He drove him
Into the ground to his waist,

And although he did not break his spine,
Kyuren Kylysh lifted his eyes to the sky:
And his pure soul departed.
Setting off at a run:
– There are probably no *alyps* left
For me to battle! – said Kёk Torchuk,
Bogatyrs with *bogatyrs,*
Fine fellows beat fine fellows.
Some of the *alyps*, mounted their horses,
While others rode facing back to front, and they fled.

-20-
After nine days, no *alyps* remained:
Everything was destroyed.
Leaving, he looks about:
An *alyp's* descendent sat
At the base of the white mountain with sixty mountain passes,
Tucking the white mountain beneath him.
He half-crushed the white mountain.
Like the white mountain himself, he sat.
– Wait, Kёk Torchuk, – he said, –
The way I see it, you are the only
Remaining true *bogatyr* in the white world!
You have killed Kuba Salgyn,
The immortal, undying,
Who filled the world with his birth!
Now I will extinguish your pure soul, – and so saying,
He stretched out his right arm,
And grasped the broad breast
Of Kёk Torchuk and pulled him close.
When he stood,
Kёk Torchuk reached only his right hand
Relative to him!
– *Eze*, – said Kёk Torchuk, –

What sort of *alyp* are you?
You, who have grabbed my broad chest,
Chest like a mountain, – he asked.
What sort of *alyp*?
I am Altyn Tas!
Upon learning about you, I came,
In order to battle with you, in order to know
Who you are,
Kĕk Torchuk, was created, – he said.
Then Kĕk Torchuk
He wanted to grip onto him, but could not catch hold,
He wanted to grasp him, but could not get a grip!
The other one battered him for almost nine days.
After nine days,
Kĕk Torchuk sees:
The hand of an *alyp* rose up
From beneath the earth.
The newly appeared *alyp*'s arm
Threw Kĕk Torchuk off to the side.
Then it grasped Altyn Tas by the chest
And disappeared beneath the land.
Seeing this, Kĕk Torchuk,
Sighed, sat down, and composed himself.
– Great trouble, great woe! – he said, –
What *alyp* was it that helped me?
Then he hears:
The call of the *alyp* rising
Up from beneath the earth:
– *Eze*, Kĕk Torchuk, brother, – he said, –
I returned
When I went down to my resting place,
And learned that you fell into the hands
Of Altyn Tas, who lost his name.
And now I am battling with Altyn Tas! –

He yelled out.

Then he hears how under the earth

An *alyp* began to beat another alyp.

The cry of the *alyp* was heard:

– No matter how you beat me, Altyn Tas, – he said, –

You cannot attain my pure soul

As I have already died, – he said, –

When your strength runs out, – he said, –

Then I will capture your pure soul! –

The other called forth.

Then Kёk Torchuk waited and waited:

He waited almost forty days.

After forty days

The *alyp* so struck the *alyp*

Under the earth –

That the seated Kёk Torchuk

Was thrown nine meters away.

Then he hears,

The call of an *alyp* rang out:

– *Eze*, brother Kёk Torchuk, – he said, –

Go to the girl

That you plan to marry and take her.

I have captured the pure soul

Of the immortal-undying Altyn Tas,

Who filled the world with his birth! – so he called out.

Seeing this,

Hearing this,

Kёk Torchuk's eyes were filled with tears:

Adanmada, Kuba Salgyn, brother,

Now you call me brother,

My brother

Has conquered the pure soul of Altyn Tas!

Look, his soul rose,

Because of me, – he said. –

Well, he dragged Altyn Tas below the earth
And there he captured his pure soul! –
So declaring, he sobs!

-21-
Then he jumped up
And went to Ak Kan's golden palace
And he went inside the golden palace.
The door having opened, he gave greeting,
Crossing the threshold, he bowed.
Ak Kan grasped him by the hand
And under the arm,
And seated him at the golden table.
– *Eze*, Ak Kan, – said Kёk Torchuk, –
Bring out your daughter, Ala Manak.
If I like her, I will take her!
And if I do not, as she has a father,
She can certainly stay in her father's land?
Having thrown wide open the doors of nine rooms,
Ak Kan called out:
– *Eze*, Ala Manak, daughter, come out here,
To Kёk Torchuk, with whom
You shall join heads, – he said, –
If you are pleasing to him, he will take your hand,
If not – as you have a father,
Will you not remain in the land of your father? – the other said.
Then he hears:
The scrape of boots echoing in the heavens.
When she stepped out –
The girl came out attended by sixty servants,
With seventy retainers –
And the golden palace was lit up with red light.
– Here, Kёk Torchuk, – he said, –
This is my daughter,

58

If you find her pleasing, carry her away!
– *Eze*, Ak Kan, – he said, –
If I won't take this sort of girl,
What sort of girl would I take?
The young people sat down nearby,
Their beauty darkened the moon,
And beyond that the sun was eclipsed.
Joining their two heads
Conducting the female wedding
For almost nine days,
They sit, they eat and drink.
After nine days
Kёk Torchuk leapt up:
– *Eze*, Ak Kan, father-in-law,
I have my own land, and I am missing it,
I have my own river, and I am weary for it!
Although it is not tall, I have my own mountain.
Although it is not deep, I have my own river, –
I will return to my land, – he said. –
Since I left the land of my father Kёk Kan,
Left the foot of the blue mountain,
I have forgotten everything! – he said.
I left there a child,
Having lived there to middle age, – he said.
Hearing this,
Ak Kan and Ak Kёzhe, his wife,
Cried
Many tears from their eyes.
Ak Kan and Ak Kёzhe, his wife,
Calling, they bellow!
– *Eze*, Kёk Torchuk, son-in-law, – he said, –
Do not forget my land,
Take care of it, do not be a stranger!
– *Eze*, father-in-law, – Kёk Torchuk said, –

From time to time I will visit!
– Dear,
Daughter, our only one,
Ala Manak, – they said, –
Will we see you again with our own two eyes?
You are taking her so far away!
You are taking her to the end of this world.
Ala Manak wiped tears
From her eyes as well.
Kĕk Torchuk grasped Ala Manak,
Crumpled and flipped her,
Turning her into a golden egg,
And placed her in his right pocket.
He parted bade farewell and bowed
To Ak Kan and Ak Kĕzhe.
When he went out of the golden palace
They followed after.
Stepping down from the golden porch
He clung to the three-eared blue-grey horse
Like a bat.
He turned,
And ascended the mountain ridge.

-22-
Having climbed the ridge,
He pressed the stirrups and spurred the horse,
And so jerked on the horse's gaping jaw,
The horse set off at a gallop;
Like a whistling golden arrow,
He galloped.
He rode and rode –
Did he ride a little or a lot?
He looked ahead:
A golden mountain with sixty passes stood ahead.

A black mountain grew again
Alongside the golden mountain with sixty passes.
Then, driving the horse a little, he sees:
The black mountain moved.
This Kёk Torchuk riding his horse
Then sees:
An *alyp* sits, like a black mountain.
– Wait, – said the *alyp*, –
A roe deer that is fated to die,
Dashed across the snow!
Like a mountain, the *alyp* said:
– The white world
Filled by the birth of Kuba Salgyn,
The immortal, undying.
You, Kёk Torchuk,
Your pure soul has been conquered,
Now I will conquer your pure soul! – he said,
Grasped him, but did not drag him
As with a child born only yesterday.
He arose, placing
Kёk Torchuk under him.
Kёk Torchuk's pure soul
Almost leapt out, as it lay there.
Blinking his eyes, he lies there.
He lies there for almost six days.
After six days
The hand of the *alyp* appeared.
It grasped the black *alyp*,
Sitting like a mountain, by the chest,
And dragged him underground.
The *alyp*'s cry carried up from under the earth:
– *Eze*, Kёk Torchuk, brother,
When I descend to the resting place,
In my resting place,

I just began to open the doors,
Thankfully, I had not managed to go in!
When I had grasped the door handle,
And began to go in,
Having learned that Kara Alyp had grasped you
And placed you beneath him,
I returned! – he said.
Then Kёk Torchuk hears:
The *bogatyr* began to beat the *bogatyr*
Beneath the earth.
The Kёk Torchuk's cry rang out:
– *Eze,* you, born Kara Alyp, are divided in two!
Like a mountain, you, Kara Alyp,
No matter how much you hit, – he said, –
My Kuba Salgyn,
Who has already left the white world,
You will not conquer his pure soul, – he says. –
When your strength wanes,
Then I will reach
Your pure soul, –
So saying, he shouted.
Hearing this, Kёk Torchuk,
Wiping tears to the side
From two eyes, he said:
– *Adanmada*, it seems that
I, Kёk Torchuk was born foolish!
Thusly born, Kuba Salgyn, brother,
Alas, I defeated his pure soul, –
So saying, he cries.
Then he waited and waited:
Almost 40 days
Alyp grasped *alyp*, fighting.
After 40 days
And then he hears:

The cry of an *alyp* from under the ground rang out:
– Wait, Kara Alyp, – it calls, –
You beat me for almost forty days!
Your pure strength waned.
Now judge the hands of Kuba Salgyn, – he said.
While Kёk Torchuk sat:
The *alyp* so beat the *alyp* –
Again Kёk Torchuk was thrown for nine meters.
Then he hears,
An *alyp* shouts:
– *Eze,* Kёk Torchuk, brother,
Now, there is no place that you shall fear!
Go home!
Now, I will descend
To my place of rest, – he said. –
And I will not return!
Then the *alyp*'s voice was silent.
Kёk Torchuk mounted
His three-eared blue-red roan horse,
Well, his blue-grey horse,
And with a shout, sobbing, returned:
– *Adanmada*, born foolish,
Look, it is I, Kёk Torchuk,
And I defeated such a brother
His pure soul! – he said.
He rode and he rode,
Ahead he then sees:
The peak of the blue mountain
With seventy passes, is already visible.

-23-

He descended into the embrace of the mountain's saddle
Along the smooth ridge
To the foot of the blue mountain,

And looked carefully about:
The livestock stand as they stood,
The people live as they lived.
Having reached the bottom,
Then Kёk Torchuk sees:
The hinged doors opened:
Kёk Torgu and Kёk Kan together, steadfast
Gone grey, like a white-harrier hawk moon, they stepped out.
– Dear Kёk Torchuk, our son, has returned! –
So saying,
They stepped down off the golden porch,
Took him off the horse,
Taking him under the arms.
They led him into the golden palace.
– *Eze*, Kёk Torchuk, son,
Since you left the foot of the blue mountain,
Much time has passed, – they said. –
Have you brought something long anticipated? – they asked.
– Yes! – he replied.
From his right pocket, he pulled out the golden egg,
And tossed it –
In place of the golden egg,
Swaying like a goose-mother,
Rousing like a gosling,
A girl leapt up.
Kёk Kan and Kёk Torgu
Walked around her, saying:
– Well, son, – they said, –
You have brought the best of girls! –
Now, our clan-family lineage
Will never be interrupted! – so saying,
They sat at the golden table.

-24-

Kёk Kan walked out of the golden palace,
Snatched up forty axes,
And summoned forty *chaizan*-shepherds:
– *Eze*, forty *chaizans*, – he said, –
Kёk Torchuk, our son,
Has brought a girl, praise the heavens!
We will put on a great wedding! – he said. –
For almost seven days
Hardly noticing day or night,
Almost nine days
Hardly noticing night or day,
Let it be a great wedding! – so saying,
He threw them forty axes.
Forty *chaizans* caught forty axes,
And ran to their livestock:
Bellowing, well-fed fillies
Shrieking young fillies they began to strike down,
They began a great wedding.
They celebrated and celebrated:
For almost seven days,
Not noticing day or night,
For almost nine days,
Not noticing night or day,
They put on a great wedding.
After nine days,
The great wedding came to an end.
They gave close relatives golden robes.
Distant relatives
Received silk robes
Those that received silk robes
Whisper:
– Look, – they say, –
We should have been given golden robes,

Others received these golden robes!
We were also close relatives, –
So they whispered amongst themselves.

-25-
After nine days,
When the great wedding was ending.
Kёk Torchuk left the golden palace
Removed the golden saddle from the
Three-eared blue-grey horse,
And threw it, like a heap!
He removed the silver bridle from the horse's head:
– *Eze*, blue-grey horse of mine, – he said, –
Go to the foot of Mount Syurgyu,
And, nibble three times, eat the grass!
Go to the shores of the milky lake,
And with three swallows, drink water! –
So saying, he released the horse. –
When I need you, I will whistle –
And you will come at a run, – so saying, he let him go.
The blue-grey horse, leaping forward, galloped off.
Kёk Torchuk turned away and
Went into the golden palace.

-26-
In their land
No strange *bogatyrs* enter with a cry,
War does not occur, nor oppression.
He became a great khan of khans,
He became a great *piy*-leader among *piys*,
He lived here.
Lyubasha, who listened to me,[13]
Let your soul travel high!
Let your life's path be long!

I went into the bushes,
I caught a white rabbit.
I loaded the good fortune of the white khan
Onto the white rabbit as it went here and there
I mounted the white rabbit,
And rode him to this land.
The catch a great khan,
Eat up, eat!
In telling the long tale – I did not lengthen,
In telling it briefly – I did not abridge,
My listener Lyubasha,
You are a great gift to me!

Chepe Salgyn and His Plain Chestnut Horse

-1-

Before today's generation lived,
After the long-ago generation lived.
It was in the time that the earth was taking shape,
Land and water were taking form.
A stirring rod divided the land,
Waters separated with a dipper.
Greening, the young grass grew.
This was in the time when on the crowns of trees
Green foliage, breaking through, grew.
On the canopy of the white birch with the golden leaves,
Forty birds chirped,
Above the green grass,
Young nightingales sang.

-2-

With sixty high passes, the white mountain stands.
At the foot of the white mountain
With sixty passes, surging,
The white sea flows.
On the shore of that white sea
White livestock grazes.
A multitude of people lives in a village.
Amidst the multitudinous village,
On the shore of the white sea,
Sparkling under the sun and moon,
Stands a golden palace.
At the golden palace,
At the golden hitching post
That cannot be uprooted by a horse,
A three-eared light-grey horse stands.

Stretched out from weakness,
The chin six *sazhens* long,[14]
The nose three *sazhens* long.
Such an aging horse stands.
Entering into the golden palace,
Opening the doors, I made greeting,
Stepping over the threshold, I bowed.
Then I see[15]
Behind the golden table,
Having survived to the third generation,[16]
Ak Kan lives here.
His wife, Altyn Aryg,
Setting out food and drink on the golden table,
Serving Ak Kan.
Getting their fill of food and drink together.
When they had feasted on food and drink,
Ak Kan said:
– *Eze*, Altyn Aryg, my wife,
I have lived to an old man's age,
Reached a third generation already.
If a strange *bogatyr-alyp*[17] enters,
Attains my pure soul,
He will steal away the white livestock we raised,
Together with our people-village.
We have reached the third generation,
But not borne a man-heir, – he said.
As he uttered those words,
The doors of the forty rooms opened wide.
Then they saw,
A girl enter –
One of her breasts was like a mountain,
The other – like a mountain.
That was the sort of girl who entered.
In nine places stomping through

The iron floor,
She entered.
Entering, she said:
– *Pai-pai*, father,
Why did you utter such bad words?
Now the words said by you,
Will ring through the world.
There is no time to sit,
My broad sides shall not lie down! – she said. –
Alyps will begin to come to our land,
In order to destroy your pure soul,
Steal away our livestock.
Have you forgotten, – she said. –
That you have Altyn Chustuk, a daughter?
As long as my head is whole,
What *alyp* can take our people and our livestock? –
Having spoken,
Altyn Chustuk sat down at the golden table.
She began to take her fill of food and drink.

-3-
When she had gotten her fill of food and drink,
The earth's surface began to shake,
The bottom of the earth swayed.[18]
– See, father, having heard your words,
The *alyp* is already coming to our land.
Throwing open the hinged window, she sees:
A flaxen-maned light-grey horse descending,
Onto the ridge where strange horses have not tread,[19]
– O, father, – she said,
This *alyp* has not traveled far.
Living not far away,
Nine worlds away from us,
Living at the foot of the golden mountain

With forty passes,
And with his flaxen-maned light grey horse,
Altyn Kylysh is coming, – she said.
He is coming to feast on our livestock in the forest.
Then they hear:
Altyn Kylysh's horse gallops with the thunder of a hundred
    horses,
And with the cry of a hundred *alyps,* the *alyp* cries:
–Ak Kan, are you home?
Come out here!
I have broken into pieces
Your graceful backbone,
I'll steal away your white livestock! –
So he yelled.
Hearing this, Altyn Chustuk, the girl,
Entered the forty rooms.
Her parents then saw:
Altyn Chustuk exit the forty rooms,
Donning a three-layered
Golden hauberk.
– Such a hauberk will even suit,
This *bogatyrka,* father, – she said,
Bowing and bidding farewell,
She left the golden palace.
Toward the descending offspring of the *alyps*
She set off into the white steppe to meet him.
She dragged him
Off the horse, grabbing the *alyp* by the collar.
– *Eze,* Altyn Kylysh, – she said, –
You came to feast on livestock not your own?
I'll pound your graceful backbone
Into pieces! – she said,
And would not let him pass.
She gathered him up in a heap from the black earth

And lifted him to the peak of the forty heavens.
When, turning away, she cast him down
Onto the earth, crushing
His backbone in nine places.
Turning on her heel
She returned to the palace:
– You see, father,
This Altyn Kylysh is a mere no one,
Who entered the forest to kill grown livestock.

-4-
Sitting down to the table
She began to take her fill of food and drink –
When the earth's surface began to sway,
And the earth's bottom shook.
And then they saw:
On the mountain ridge, where strange horses do not tread,
Older-Younger, at a height of nine sazhens,
Gray-sorrel horses descended.
– See, Father,
True *alyps* have begun to come.
From the mountain ridge
With the clatter of a hundred horses they gallop,
Shouting with the cries of a hundred *alyps*:
– *Eze*, Ak Kan, are you home?
If you are a *bogatyr* – we duel,
If you are a fighter – we battle, come out!
We have come to steal away your white livestock! –
They called.
Altyn Chustuk dashed out from behind the golden table.
And headed for the door.
Leaving the golden palace,
Stepping down from the golden porch,
She set out to meet them.

They set out to meet each other on the white steppe.
When they were in the white steppe,
Seizing one *alyp* with her right hand,
And the other, with her left,
By the breast,
She pulled them from the horses.
Having pulled them from the horses,
She battled the two bogatyrs.
They struggled for three days:
An impenetrable pitch black
Fog fell.
After three days
Altyn Chustuk gathered from the black earth
The two *bogatyrs* into a heap.
She swung them to the forty heavens,
And turning, she so cast them down –
That their bony bits were broken
In nine places, she beat them so.
Older-younger
Grey-sorrel horses wanted to flee,
She grabbed them by their tails,
One with her right hand, the other with her left,
And so shook
That the bloodied bodies of the horses
Tumbled with a cry to the nine heavens,
Their spirits left them there.
– If you came with the *alyps*
Together to this pure land,
You will die together, as you traveled together, –
Having said that, Altyn Chustuk
Turned away,
And walked into the golden palace.
Walking into the golden palace:
– See, father,

Because of your words
Now there is no time to sit,
No time to lie on broad sides, – she advised.

-5-
When, having sat, and partaken
Of food and drink,
The land swayed this way,
That way.
– Whatever happened? –
Saying so, they looked:
On the mountain ridge where strange horses do not tread,
Nine pairs
Of moon-sorrel horses descending.
Atop these nine pairs
Of moon-sorrel horses
Lay a raft made of iron.
On that iron raft,
Lay a girl on a mat.
With the thunder of a hundred horses they galloped,
With the shouts of a hundred *alyps*, she yelled:
– *Eze*, are you in the golden palace,
Altyn Chustuk, who spars
With the fellows on the sporting field,
Strolling with nine fellows,
With two breasts like two mountains
Spreading out? –
Come out here,
I will crush your
Graceful backbone into pieces, –
Called out the girl.
Seeing this, Altyn Chustuk,
Ran into the forty rooms.
Having run into the forty rooms,

When she came out, her father and mother see:
She set out after donning chainmail
Of forty layers.
– See, father,
The best *bogatyr* of the *alyps* is coming.
This girl –
With the lost name and forty breasts
Kydai Aryg enters.
Not simple, this Kydai Aryg!
She lives
Below seventy layers of earth.
Lo, that *bogatyrka*-girl arrived,
On whom I must spend my strength, – said
Altyn Chustuk, calling from the golden window:
– Strolling with the forty fellows on the sporting field,
Walking with forty fellows,
She removed her two breasts,
Kydai Aryg who has grown forty breasts, –
So saying, from whence she spoke her voice.
– Come down here, and when I step out,
I will crush your graceful backbone
Into pieces,
Kydai Aryg of the forty breasts! –
So saying, Altyn Chustuk yelled.
Kydai Aryg, descending from there,
Called out and descended:
– For ninety games
Her two breasts, like two mountains, spreading,
Altyn Chustuk, come out here!
Altyn Chustuk, bowing and bidding farewell to her parents,
Began to leave the golden palace.
– Father, this is the *bogatyrka*,
To whom I must give my strength, she has come, – so saying,
She stepped off the golden porch,

Walking out to meet her.
When nine pairs of moon-chestnut horses
Walked toward her,
The girl, lying
On the edge of the iron raft, sprang up,
And jumped from the iron raft,
Landing knee-deep
Sprawling on the black earth.
Then she took hold of her breasts,
And they began to battle,
An impenetrable pitch black
Fog fell.
When they crashed against the black cliffs
Of the white mountain –
The black mountain rained down loose rock.
When they approached the white sea,
Turning the white sea to mud
From their battle, they struggled.
They battled, they fought.
Mightily, quietly, they fought:
They battled for forty days.
After forty days
Altyn Chustuk, shouting,
And pulled to her
The forty-breasted Altyn Aryg,
And set her on her hands and knees.
– What, Kydai Aryg,
When you landed in my arms,
Never dream again, – she said,
Of traveling the white world.
She drove her up the slope
She drove her down the slope.
Grasping her,
The forty-breasted Kydai Aryg,

And dropping her arms,
As if they were lead, she fell tumbling
Under the black earth.
Nine pairs of moon-sorrel horses,
Turned away and fled.
– Wait, Kydai Aryg, – she said, –
When you run, dropping like lead,
Where are you running from me?
Digging into the earth, you cannot get in,
Had you wings, you could not reach the sky-god! –
So said Altyn Chustuk, and she turned and ran.
She untied the nine-times tied
Dilapidated light grey horse of her father.

-6-
Like a bat, she clung to him,
The unhitched light grey horse.
Turning, Altyn Chustuk
Drove the horse up the mountain ridge.
When she reached the ridge top,
She pressed the stirrups,
And spurred the horse on –
The light grey horse set off at a gallop.
Ran-ran,
A long time, or a little, the horse ran –
He ran to an opening-*tyundyuk*[20] in the earth.
She drove the horse through the opening-*tyundyuk* into the earth.
She went down and down,
A little, a lot, she went down –
Under seventy layers of earth she went.
Black shadows spread there.
Altyn Chustuk then saw:
Beyond those seventy layers of earth,
Circling down the earth,

A winged black city stood.
At the foot of the winged black city
Stood a black building having seventy corners.
Nine moon-sorrel horses stood there.
Seeing this, Altyn Chustuk
Galloped with the thunder of a hundred horses,
Calling with the voice of a hundred *alyps*:
– *Eze*, forty-breasted Kydai Aryg,
Walking with forty fellows on the sporting field,
Losing forty of her breasts,
Kydai Aryg, come out here!
I will crush your graceful backbone
Into pieces! –
So calling, Altyn Chustuk saw that
The hinged doors flew open,
And the forty-breasted Kydai Aryg
Scowled like a black mountain as she came out.
– Wait, Altyn Chustuk,
Since you have come to my land,
There's no choice:
I will take you off this white world! – she threatened.
When she leaped from the iron porch,
She sank to her waist in the black earth.
From there she jumped
Onto the earth
And ran to meet her.
When she approached,
Altyn Chustuk leapt from the horse.
Meeting, they grabbed breasts,
As they began to battle
An impenetrable pitch-black
Fog fell.
They fought for forty days.
After forty days

Altyn Chustuk yelled,
And so wrenched Kydai Aryg,
That she set her on her hands and knees.
– Wait, Kydai Aryg, – she said, –
Not long ago, you
Turned to lead and descended?
Now you cannot escape my grasp, – so saying,
She began to drag the *bogatyrka* up the slope
And knocked her down the slope,
Pulling her to the left side, to the right,
And began to lift her off the black earth.
Kydai Aryg broke through three layers of earth with her legs.
Pulling her legs out of the black earth,
Lifted from there over nine layers of earth.
Then, unwinding, she struck so hard –
That the earth, created by god,
Swayed like a black cradle.
Altyn Chustuk then saw:
Kydai Aryg sink on the left,
Through seven layers of earth,
Although her backbone did not break,
Her pure soul left, and she died.
From there, Altyn Chustuk went,
She entered the black house.
No one was there.
She up-ended all in the black house,
Spread a sea of ashes,
Broke black pots,
Overturned everything.
She left the black house.
And clung to the light-grey horse
Like a bat.
Turning the horse, then
She drove the horse

Away from there, up to the earth.

-7-

She climbed and climbed:
Climbed to the world of the sun.
From there, onward to the white mountain
With sixty mountain passes she rode.
He sank into the embrace of the mountain's saddle,
Descending along the smooth ridge
To the foot of the white mountain,
When she looked closely:
People lived as they lived,
Livestock grazed as they grazed.
They lived.
– *Che*, while I was gone
The *bogatyrs* did not come! – she said. –
Now the *alyp* will not come.
Now that I have defeated the pure soul that lost its name,
The undying-immortal
Forty-breasted Kydai Aryg,
Which *alyp*,
Fearing me, will come?
She descended, setting loose
The light grey horse near the golden hitching post,
And entered the golden palace.
Opening the doors, she gave greeting,
Crossing the threshold, she bowed.
– Greetings, Ak Kan, father,
And Altyn Aryg, mother dear, – she said.
– Hello, hello, dearest, – they said,
Taking her by the arms,
Supporting under her arms,
They seated her at the golden table.
Altyn Aryg, running,

Served her food and drink.
Altyn Chustuk did not set aside the cup –
She was hungry!
Large bones flew out of her mouth,
Small bones flew from her nostrils.
Spoon on top, press with the spoon,
That's how you eat!
As they ate,
They ate for six days.
After six days,
Through the hinged windows
An iron swallow flew in.
Having arrived, the iron swallow
Sprawled on the golden table.
And they saw:
Under its right wing
An urgent letter lay.
When they took the urgent letter,
Altyn Chustuk read it.
The upper creator wrote thusly:
– *Eze*, Altyn Chustuk, we here
Nine creators have organized a contest!
Nine creators of the black mountain
Created a black *bogatyr* with
The strength of seventy *bogatyrs*, created
To battle with you.
I have put you forward.
The nine creators made Kara Alyp.
Rise up immediately today! – He wrote. –
If you do not come up here today,
You will be turned into a maiden-stone! –
So he wrote.
Upon reading this, Altyn Chustuk:
– *Eze*, Ak Kan, Father, – she said, –

You see, the sole creator
Has sent me an urgent letter,
Asking me to come.
If I do not go up there,
As a girl, I will be turned to stone, – she said.
– *Eze*, child, there is no getting away
From the only creator!
You must go up, said the father.
Hearing this, Altyn Chustuk
Leapt from behind the golden table,
And bowed and bade farewell to
Ak Kan, her father, and to Altyn Aryg, her mother,
She left the golden palace.
She nestled like a bat
Against her father's aging light grey horse.
Then, turning away,
She raced to the mountain ridge.

-8-
From there she rode hard to the middle of the earth,
To the golden mountain,
With seventy mountain passes
Growing up to the heavens, she arrived.
At the peak of the golden mountain
With the seventy passes,
And having reached there,
She began to climb to
The seventy heavens.
When she reached the seventy heavens,
Altyn Chustuk sees:
The same land, the same sun.
At the peak of the seventy heavens
Were the same mountains, golden.
In the land of the sole creator,

The golden mountain with forty passes,
Pressed into one corner,
Alyps from the sunny side –
All *alyps* from the sunny world –
Sat gathered here.
When Altyn Chustuk, crossing
Over the mountain ridge, rode,
Whistling back and forth, they yelled.
Whispering to each other, they said:
– The white world was illuminated by her birth,
Undying, immortal
Daughter of Ak Kan,
Altyn Chustuk, entered, – they whispered. –
Look, friends, – they said, –
One of her breasts is like a mountain,
The other like a mountain, that girl, –
So saying, they whispered.
Altyn Chustuk heard them out.
Going down, she saw:
Eh, at the foot of the golden mountain,
She thought there was a black mountain,
Like a black mountain, the *alyp* sat.
Crushing the black mountain,
Beneath as he sat.
– Eh, Kara Alyp, made from the black mountain,
With the strength of seventy *alyps*, – she said,
Altyn Chustuk leapt from the horse,
And approached Kara Alyp.
Approaching him, she said:
– Is it you, Kara Alyp,
Made from the black mountain,
With the strength of seventy *alyps*? – she said,
Stretching out her right arm,
And grabbing his breast,

She so shook him –
And threw him over her right shoulder
Into the white steppe.
Then turning, she saw:
A shining palace stood.
Not touching, six sazhens above the black earth,
It stood, shimmering.
Approaching the shining palace, Altyn Chustuk,
So leapt,
Onto the golden porch
That the shining palace sank down.
Opening the doors, she gave greeting,
And saw:
Behind the golden table
Sat the sole creator at the far end,
All by himself.
Nine creators sat
Around the golden table.
When Altyn Chustuk came,
The doors opened, and she gave greeting,
She saw:
The wife of the sole creator,
Altyn Kas-woman, running:
– *Alas*, Altyn Chustuk, daughter, has come, – she said,
Taking her by the right hand,
Seated her at the golden table.
– Sit, take your fill of food and drink, child! – she said.
The girl sat,
Alongside the sole creator,
Sharing food and drink, she said:
– *Eze*, sole creator,
You sent me an urgent letter that you wrote.
And I have ascended.
– Good, good, Altyn Chustuk, child,

Here the nine creators made
Kara Alyp with the strength of seventy *bogatyrs*,
Made him from the black mountain.
To battle with you, they made him.
I called you out, child! – he said.
– Good, good, sole creator
Who has made me, sole creator!
Battle, I would battle,
But as I am a girl, I will not fight.
If I am turned into a man,
Then I will battle, – she said.
Altyn Kas, having run forward,
She clapped her on the right shoulder:
– Aha, very smart, clever,
You are, Altyn Chustuk, child!
She said truly.
Well, sole creator,
How can she, being a girl, fight?
Turn Altyn Chustuk, daughter,
Into a man, – she said.
The sole creator looked that way,
Looked this way:
What choice do I have?
I will turn the girl Altyn Chustuk
Into a man, – he said.
– *Eze*, Altyn Kas, wife,
Pour daughter Altyn Chustuk some wine.
O, Altyn Kas, hearing this,
Turned away
And went into the nine rooms.
When she came out of the nine rooms:
She poured wine into
The golden cup which
Sixty *alyps* cannot drink dry and said:

– See, child, give the sole creator
Wine from your own hand, – she said.

-9-
Altyn Chustuk jumped up
Grasped the golden cup:
– *Eze*, sole creator
Who made me, sole creator,
Take this wine and partake, and
Transform me, a girl,
Into a man, – she said.
The sole creator stood,
When he began to drink from the golden cup,
As if it were the white sea, the wine seethed,
As it poured into his mouth.
When he had drunk the wine
He was so drunk his whiskers bristled wide.
– *Oh*, Altyn Kas, my wife,
Has made strong wine.
Well, child,
Let us go out on the golden porch!
When they were on the golden porch,
The sole creator began to shout:
– Let all with ears hear! –
Let all with eyes see! –
I will turn into a man
Daughter Altyn Chustuk, – so saying, he shouted.
The name that I will pronounce,
Let it reach from the white world, created by god,
To the two seventy worlds.
Let it reach to the Lower World,
To the khanate of the nine Erlik-khans, – he said.
Let it reach my Upper World,
Reach to the sole creator.

If there is to be a name, let it be a name.
Is there is not to be a name, let the whirlwind sweep it away.
Your father – Ak Kan,
Altyn Aryg – your mother!
Let your plain chestnut horse
Never
Be passed by another horse!
Let the plain chestnut horse be so.
Riding on the plain chestnut horse,
Not submitting to other *alyps*,
Undying, immortal
Chepe Salgyn you will be! –
Thus the sole creator shouted.
– Now child,
Go into the palace,
So that your name will take hold, sleep, – he said.
Altyn Kas ran up:
– Come here,
Chepe Salgyn, child, – she said,
And took her by the arm,
Brought her into the nine rooms.
Took her into the nine rooms,
And laid her on the golden bed:
– Sleep now, son, – she said. –
During the night, your peace ensuring,
During the day, your dreams protecting,
I will watch over you! – she said,
And sat nearby.
And thus he went to sleep!
Chepe Salgyn slept and slept:
Three days they waited, and he did not awaken,
Six days they waited, and he did not awaken.
On the ninth day,
Playing, dawn began,

Shining, the sun rose.
And they saw:
A little fellow, stretching, began to awaken.
He stretched his legs
From the near corner to the very doors.
When he sprung up,
The shining palace began to rock to and fro.
– Oh, child, very good:
Now you have become a man.
Adanmada, you have become
The best of men, child!
Let us go out, – proposed Altyn Kas.
They went into the nine rooms.
There, the sole creator together
With the nine creators, mouths agape, looked:
He had become an *alyp* like a mountain.
Leaving the golden palace,
Chepe Salgyn saw:
Alongside the light grey horse,
A wonderful plain chestnut horse stood.
The flame from his eyes
Burned the grass to its roots.
Steam rushed from his two nostrils –
Look how he stands!
– Look, son, the plain
Chestnut horse that you will ride.
You see, the horse that was created?
– I see, Altyn Kas, – so saying,
He went into the golden palace.
Sitting behind the golden table,
Chepe Salgyn said:
– *Che*, nine creators,
Let me partake of food and drink,
And then, I will go out

And battle the *alyp* with the strength of seventy *bogatyrs*.
He sat, for an entire six days,
And took his fill of food and drink.
When he was sated with food and drink,
– Let us go out! – he commanded,
And they began to leave the golden palace.

-10-
When they left the golden palace,
Chepe Salgyn so sprang from the golden porch,
That he sunk to his waist.
Jumping onto the ground,
He approached Kara Alyp.
Kara Alyp sat there like a mountain.
Chepe Salgyn walked up to him,
And grabbing for his breast,
So wrenched him that he arose.
– Wait, Kara Alyp, – Altyn Kas said, –
You and Kara Alyp,
With the strength of seventy *bogatyrs*,
When you fall into the hands of Chepe Salgyn,
You will no longer travel the white world! – he said.
And thus, grappling,
They battled:
An impenetrable pitch-black
Fog fell.
Did they fight a little, did they fight long?
Month after month flew by, a year passed.
When they came to themselves:
As it transpired, six years they battled.
They learned, from the sun baking their crowns,
That summer had come.
They learned, from the hoar frost falling on their heads,
That winter had come.

After six years
Chepe Salgyn, shouting, so shook Kara Alyp
With the strength of seventy *bogatyrs*,
That he fell to his hands and knees.
– Wait, Kara Alyp, how do you think
You will escape from my grasp? – he said,
He began to drive him up the slope,
He dragged him down the slope.
Like a black belt, he twisted him,
Like a black sack, he shook him.
Pulling him to the right-left flank,
Pulled him from the black earth.
And then he saw
This Kara Alyp
Pierced six layers of earth.
Tossing him, he dragged and dragged:
Pulled his legs from the black earth.
And then began to lift him upward.
Lifting him to the forty heavens,
He spun,
And then so struck him –
That the white world, made by the creator,
Swayed as a black cradle.
And then he saw:
The *alyps* swarming the golden mountain
With forty mountain passes,
Like black deadwood,
They tumbled down the golden mountain.
When they began to look for Kara Alyp –
In the end he was driven deep
Into the seventh layers of earth.
Kara Alyp's backbone was unbroken,
His pure soul so left:
Glancing at the seventy heavens,

His pure soul left him.

-11-

When Chepe Salgyn, turning,
Went into the golden palace,
He hears:
The shout of the sole creator,
Carrying forth:
– Did you see, nine creators? – he said, -
Having chosen to compete with me,
Now you will be
My servant!
The nine creators, lowering their eyes,
Did not ascend, they stood.
Chepe Salgyn, approaching,
Stepped onto the golden porch,
– Hello, sole creator,
Creator who made me, – he said,
And shook his right hand.
– Aha, child, hello-hello,
Let's go into the golden palace! – answered the creator.
When they entered the golden palace,
They sat around the golden table of the creator.
The sole creator
Sat alongside Chepe Salgyn.
Altyn Kas, patting Chepe Salgyn on the back,
– Dear Chepe Salgyn, son,
Now who will you have
To fear on the whole white world? – she said. –
There is no one on this white world for you to fear.
When all sat and partook of food and drink,
The sole creator said:
– *Che,* the nine creators, now
Go to your golden palaces and

Bring the rest of the people.
Here, having become my servants,
You will serve me;
Having become my slaves,
You will attend me.
Hearing this, Chepe Salgyn said:
– *Eze*, sole creator,
Sole creator that made me,
How will you turn these nine creators
Into servants?
They are creators, as are you.
I gave my strength,
Let them cease battling with you.
If they promise,
Then, let the creators live on
As they have before.
I gave my strength!
As I say, so shall it be.
If I say that they will be servants –
Then they will live like servants.
I gave my strength.
Let the nine creators,
As they were creators, so they continue to live.
But let them stop fighting with you,
Let them cease battling with you.
Do you hear, nine creators?
We heard, we heard, Chepe Salgyn.
Aha, very smart,
You are very wise, Chepe Salgyn!
With the sole creator-*chaiachy*, – they promised,
We will no longer battle, – they promised.
– Did you hear, sole creator? – asked Chepe Salgyn;
– I heard! – he answered.
– So, as you were creators-*chaiachy*, so you shall live,

Fight no longer with the sole creator!
– We will not fight, Chepe Salgyn! – they swore.
Then Chepe Salgyn in the golden palace
Partook of food and drink....
It seems, Chepe Salgyn,
Having bridled the light grey horse
He sent him below.
– When you reach the land of the father, stand there!
Having so spoken, he sent him.
... After six days,
When he had partaken of food and drink, he leapt up,
– *Eze*, sole creator, – he said, –
Although it is not tall, my mountain stands.
Although it is not deep, my river flows.
— I have my own land – and I miss it,
I have my own river – and I am weary for it! –
I am returning to my land!
– Go back, go back, child! – said the creator.
Altyn Kas, running ahead of him, said:
– *Eze*, Chepe Salgyn, have no fear now.
Do not fear anything,
There is no land where you need be afraid, – and having said so,
She conducted him out of the golden palace,
Leading him by the hand.
When Chepe Salgyn left the golden palace,
All the creators left with him.
Parting ways, bowing,
He stepped down off the golden porch,
Over to the plain chestnut horse
And clung to the horse as does a bat.
Then Chepe Salgyn saw:
All the *alyps* of the earth had gathered here,
Looking out for him, awaiting him.
When he left,

The *alyps* so shouted,
That it was heard throughout the land:
– On this white earth, – they shouted, –
If a horse is born and grows,
Let the horse born
Mature into a similar plain chestnut horse;
If a man is born, and grows up,
Let the man born
Grow to be like Chepe Salgyn! – they shouted. –
An *alyp*, with the strength of seventy *bogatyrs*,
Was not born human.
You, Chepe Salgyn, were able to defeat
An *alyp* made from the black mountain! –
So they shouted.

-12-
From there, Chepe Salgyn,
Climbed to the mountain ridge,
And then galloped down –
To his land along the smooth ridge
Descending into the embrace of the mountain's saddle.
Descending,
Chepe Salgyn sees:
A light grey horse standing at the hitching post.
Black sweat dripping from it.
A hard-won road!
When he descended,
The doors of the golden palace opened.
Ak Kan and Altyn Aryg came out:
– Dear child, a daughter,
Altyn Chustuk, left us,
While Chepe Salgyn returned,
Undying, immortal,
Filling the white world with his birth, – they said,

Stepping off the golden porch,
They took him by the hands,
Under his arms,
Taking him off the horse.
They led him from either side,
Into the golden palace.
– Dear, purely created son of ours! –
So saying, they led him
And seated him at the golden table,
And began to give him food and drink.
As they gave him food and drink,
Chepe Salgyn says:
– *Eze*, Ak Kan, father,
And Altyn Aryg, mother dear,
The girl I am to marry,
Where does she live? – he asked.
– Wait, child, – Altyn Aryg said.
In the nine rooms,
In my nine-layered golden trunk,
Lies a golden book, –
I will go there to look.
When she went into the nine rooms,
The groaning of the golden trunk as it opened,
Carried throughout the palace.
When she came out,
She brought out the nine-layered golden book.
Placing the nine-layered golden book
On the golden table,
They began to read the fearsome lines.
They read and read,
And there was written:
"From here beyond the seventy worlds,
Beyond the seventy khanates
There is a sky is supported by a black mountain,

With eighty mountain passes,
And with three doors! –
That was written.
When you enter the middle door of
The black mountain with three doors:
There in the white world filled by his birth,
Undying, immortal
Kazyr Kan lives!
The undying, immortal
Kazyr Kan has three daughters!
Those three girls do not bow to the sole creator,
They do not bow before Erlik-khan,
The names of those three girls
Kazyr Tek, Tebir Tek, and Kazyr Këk! –
Were so written.
The youngest of them, Kazyr Këk,
You should take!" –
So it was written.
Having read this to Chepe Salgyn,
And having tired of waiting for him,
It seemed as if a cuckoo began to sing:
– *Eze*, Ak Kan, father,
Altyn Aryg, mother, – Chepe Salgyn said. –
Why am I lounging about here?
I will travel to the necessary place
After the girl whom I am to marry, – so saying,
Chepe Salgyn jumped up;
And bowing and bidding farewell, he said:
– If I do not return in sixty years,
It will mean I have already perished!
If I do not return in fifty years,
It means I have died! – Chepe Salgyn having said,
And bowed and bade farewell.
Leaving the golden palace,

He untied the plain chestnut horse,
And clung to it like a bat.

-13-

When he ascended the mountain ridge,
He pressed the stirrups and spurred the horse,
Which jumping forward, galloped off –
To that land.
A black fog fell,
That would not clear for nine days!
Like an arrow, golden, whistling,
Like an arrow, ringing, flies!
Chepe Salgyn rode and rode –
Did he ride a little, did he ride a lot?
Tell me quickly,
He nevertheless rode long.[21]
Having made seven gallops,
Beyond seventy worlds
It seemed he had descended.
Finding himself beyond seventy worlds,
He sees:
The black mountain supporting the sky,
With eighty mountain passes,
With three doors, appeared.
And then he heard:
At the foot of the black mountain
The call of the *alyp* carried around the whole world.
On the mountain ridge, not rushing to climb,
Hiding, Chepe Salgyn sees:
At the foot of the mountain with three doors,
The *alyps* of the sunny world,
The black *aina*-demons of the Lower World – no one remained –
Had all gathered here.
Alyp battled with *alyp*.

Chepe Salgyn watched:
Among the *alyps* three girls battled.
Alyps atop *alyp,*
One *bogatyr* walked, beating.
Then he hears,
One girl shouted:
– *Eze*, Tebir Tek and Tebir Kĕk,
How are you?
Until Chepe Salgyn,
Comes,
Filling the white world with his birth,
We must destroy *alyps*!
Seeing this, Chepe Salgyn,
Fearless, was afraid.
Unworried, began to worry.
– *Adanmada*, extraordinary girls!
Then he pulled three hairs from his head.
When he pulled the three hairs,
And thrice spitting phlegm on them, he tossed them –
A different plain chestnut horse appeared.
He took the plain chestnut horse by the reins,
Another Chepe Salgyn appeared.
– So, my creation, Chepe Salgyn, – he said, –
You will battle the *alyps* who have come!
Chepe Salgyn clung to the plain chestnut horse
Like a bat.
As he descended,
Three girls watched with their mouths agape.
– Look, Chepe Salgyn is coming
Who filled the white world with his birth! – they said!
Now, without fear, we will battle!
Thus they shouted to one another.
He, having descended,
Leapt from his horse.

The *Alyp* that cannot be held by nine embraces,
Named Kara Alyp, sat.
Approaching, Chepe Salgyn,
Grasped Kara Alyp by the chest,
And wrenched him so that he arose.
Together, they grasped each other,
And so began to fight:
An impenetrable pitch black
Fog fell.
The true Chepe Salgyn, bending over, looks about.
Then he sees:
The Chepe Salgyn he created
Battling with Kara Alyp,
For six days.
After six days
In the black fog
Oh, *bogatyr* rained blows on *bogatyr*!
Then Chepe Salgyn sees:
Kara Alyp departed,
The *alyp* that nine embraces cannot grasp.
When Kara Alyp left,
These three girls, with mouths agape, saw.
Kazyr Tek yelled in her full voice:
– Great woe, great sorrow, sisters! –
When the creator was creating Chepe Salgyn,
It was audible around the world
That Chepe Salgyn would be
Immortal and undying, so it was said!
But he did not have sufficient strength for Kara Alyp,
Despite only fighting with him for six days.
What has happened with Chepe Salgyn? –
They shouted. –
We will not let a single
Alyp escape our land alive,

We will destroy them! – So saying, they shouted. –
Since Chepe Salgyn has left the white world!
And the three girls
Began to beat the *alyps*.
The true Chepe Salgyn leapt up,
To mount the plain chestnut horse
And clung to it like a bat,
As he began to descend,
These three girls, open-mouthed,
Began to look intently.
– Great trouble, great woe! – they exclaimed, –
Behold, Chepe Salgyn is coming.
Chepe Salgyn descended,
To that Kara Alyp,
He rode toward him whom nine cannot grasp,
Leapt from the horse,
And grasped his breast.
He did not act like a child
Born only yesterday!
He did not permit him to
Step around him even six times.
Lifting him to the forty heavens,
And then turning away, he so heaved him:
That Kara Alyp's backbone
Was crushed in nine places.
Seeing this, the three girls shouted:
– There he is, the true Chepe Salgyn!
Who was the first Chepe Salgyn that entered? –
So saying, they shout.
Here is the true Chepe Salgyn, coming in!
Seeing this, the *alyps'* descendants
Seated back-to-front on their horses,
Began to gallop, fleeing.
– The undying immortal

Chepe Salgyn has come! – so saying, they shout.
Then Chepe Salgyn saw:
Only the *bogatyrs* with whom the girls battled
Remained here:
The rest had fled.

-14-
The three girls, having destroyed the *bogatyrs,*
Ran up to him and began to shout.
The eldest shouts:
– This is Chepe Salgyn whom
I will marry, he has come! – she shouts.
The middle sister approached and shouts:
– No, I will marry Chepe Salgyn!
The youngest, running forward, said:
– No, our heads have been joined together.
This is Chepe Salgyn,
I will marry him; he has come!
Thus the three girls argued amongst themselves.
They argued and argued:
Chepe Salgyn stood, observed.
Then the girls took him from both sides,
And led him into the iron mountain.
When they had led him into the iron mountain –
Inside was the same sun, the same moon, shining.
The white livestock and the populous
People-village were situated,
Chepe Salgyn sees:
A golden palace stands.
At the golden palace
At the golden hitching post that cannot be uprooted by a horse,
A wonderful horse, transcending other horses,
A three-eared
Fast, grey, three-eared horse was tied.

Bursting through three layers of this earth,
So he stands.
They led Chepe Salgyn into the golden palace.
When they led him into the golden palace,
He gave greeting when he opened the door.
Crossing the threshold, he bowed.
Seeing next, behind the golden table,
The descendant of the *bogatyrs* was sitting,
Like a black mountain, he was sitting.
He filled the entire golden table.
– So, father,
Having filled the white world with his birth,
We have brought Chepe Salgyn
The undying and immortal! – they said.
The eldest shouts:
– I will marry him!
The middle sister shouts:
– No, I will marry him!
The youngest sister, Tebir Kĕk,
Said, – No I will marry him!
They grasped the *bogatyr* from three sides,
And seated him at the golden table.
Having seated him at the golden table,
Kazyr Kĕk, the khan's wife, running,
Lay food and drink before Chepe Salgyn.
Kazyr Kan, looking at him, asked:
– *Eze*, do you see, Chepe Salgyn,
Whose birth filled the white world,
Undying, immortal,
What sorts of daughters I have?
And I myself was once Kazyr Kan, Kazyr Kan!
But I could not pacify them.
It is not simple to manage such girls.
They will not bow to the sole creator,

They will not submit to Erlik-khan, such daughters.
In marrying one of the daughters,
How will you live?
– Worry not, Kazyr Kan! – answered Chepe Salgyn. –
The girl whom I will marry is
Kazyr Kёk! – he announced. –
She is the youngest.
It is her I will take.
The three girls who shared him,
Hearing this, went quiet.
– *Eze*, Kazyr Kёk, come here,
Sit, – Chepe Salgyn beckoned. –
Having named and glorified you, it is you I will marry.
Hearing this, Kazyr Kёk
Approached, and sat alongside him.
– I know, Chepe Salgyn,
My sisters will share my place.
Our two heads shall be united!
The two of us will marry!
Hearing this, the sisters said:
– Truth, sister!
Eze, father-mother, their two heads
Must be united, – they said.
– Be seated! – commanded the parents,
Ahead, the young ones will darken the moon in the face of their
    beauty![22]
To the rear, they will darken the sun!
In joining their two heads,
We will have a big wedding celebration here.
For seven days,
Without noticing the nighttime earth,
For nine days,
Not feeling the nighttime soil, they will make merry.
After nine days, Chepe Salgyn arose:

– I have my own land – and I miss it,
I have my own river – and I am weary for it! –
And bowing and bidding farewell, he decided to return home.
Chepe Salgyn, leaving the golden palace,
And before mounting his plain chestnut horse
And clinging like a bat,
He turned the girl into a golden egg,
And placed it in his right pocket.
He clung to the plain chestnut horse
Like a bat,
And turned away the horse,
And began to ride out from the black mountain.

-15-
Leaving the black mountain,
He climbed the smooth ridge.
He so pressed the stirrups, spurring the stallion,
The horse, jumping ahead, so ran –
Like a bullet, golden and whistling,
Like an arrow, ringing, as it flew!
So rode and rode Chepe Salgyn:
Sinking into the embrace of the mountain's saddle,
On his land, along the smooth ridge
In seven gallops.
Looking about, he saw,
People living as they had lived;
Livestock grazing as it had grazed.
When he descended to the golden porch,
Chepe Salgyn saw,
The hinged doors fly open.
Father Ak Kan with Mother Altyn Aryg,
Walking out to meet him.
Dismounting the horse,
He greeted them and bowed,

Stepping onto the golden porch,
He entered the golden palace:
– *Eze,* son, if you have brought the long-awaited thing,
Show us, – they begged him.
From his right pocket
Chepe Salgyn pulled out the golden egg,
And flipped it to them:
Like a gosling-child, bestirring itself,
Like a goose, shaking,
The maiden arose.
The parents walked around her, looking:
– Well, son,
You have brought a beautiful girl.
Now our family-clan will be continued!
Chepe Salgyn and Kazyr Kёk
Were seated at the golden table,
Food and drink laid out,
And they began to serve them.
They sat around the table, talking about today,
Reminiscing about the past,
They began, while talking, to eat.
Six days they ate.
And, when they had eaten,
Altyn Aryg, mother, said:
– *Eze,* son, if you have brought a girl,
We must put on a great wedding!
And then she went outside
And standing on the porch, she shouted:
– Forty *chaizan*-shepherds, come here!
Forty *chaizans* ran to them.
Altyn Aryg tossed them forty axes:
– Slaughter all the livestock,
Prepare a big wedding!
And no sooner had they heard!

They grasped forty axes –
The well-fed livestock answered with a shout
The young livestock answered with a bellow, came running.
And they slaughtered the well-fed livestock.
For seven days,
Without noticing the nighttime earth,
They put on a great wedding,
For nine days,
Not noticing the nights,
They put on a great wedding!
After nine days,
When the great wedding had ended,
The close relatives
Were given golden robes.
Distant relatives were given
Silken robes.
Silken robes were knitted
They whisper:
– Look here, – they say, –
We should have been given golden robes,
Those are close relatives,
And were given golden robes! –
So saying, they became angry.
When the great wedding ended,
Chepe Salgyn grasped Tebir Kёk
And led her inside the nine rooms.
There they slept for nine days,
After nine days,
When they left,
Their eyes were sunken, when they came out.

-16-
Sitting, they began to partake of food and drink.
They drank and they ate,

Would they live for a little while or a long while?
The surface of the earth swayed,
The bottom of the earth shook.
– What *bogatyr* is coming? – they were surprised,
And opening the hinged windows,
Chepe Salgyn sees:
On the mountain ridge
A fast three-eared grey horse was descending.
The saddle on him was upside down,
The reins dragged on the ground.
The horse ran to the golden porch.
Seeing this, Chepe Salgyn came out:
– *Pai-pai*, fast grey horse,
Where did you throw your stalwart man,
Where did you acquire the saddle loaded upon you? –
Asked Chepe Salgyn.
– Do not even ask, Chepe Salgyn! –
It would be better if you came to our land,
To our land of the Oldest-Youngest
Shemeldei-demons have come!
The Older-Younger *Shemeldei*-demons, having come,
With sixty sorcerous spells,
And seventy tricks,
They defeated the pure souls of the sisters,
Kazyr Tek and Tebir Tek, as well as their father, Kazyr Kan! –
    He said.
– *Pai-pai*, how is it
That their pure souls were defeated?
– How were they killed?
When they ran out of the golden palace,
Into the white steppe, hidden from sight,
The *Shemeldei*-demons made rawhide straps.
They ensnared them in these rawhide straps,
And defeated their pure souls.

Hearing this, the face of Chepe Salgyn,
Redder than blood,
Turned black as liver.
His face, redder than flame,
Turned into a dead liver.
Kazyr Kĕk, hearing this,
Wiped the tears from her eyes,
Began to wail:
– Dear sisters, dear father,
It seems you have been defeated!
Eze, Chepe Salgyn,
Had I a horse, I would set out with you.
– I will go alone,
I will kill the souls of these *Shemeldei*-demons, – so saying,
Chepe Salgyn went up into the golden palace.
Took the nine-layered golden hauberk
From its hanger,
And so threw it on his shoulders,
That the entire golden palace shook.
He buttoned nine buttons,
Bowing and bidding farewell.
When he left the golden palace,
Altyn Aryg, his mother, said:
– *Eze*, son, before you leave,
Listen!
When you to the Older-Younger *Shemeldei*-demons
Will go, calling them out,
Know that they already await you.
Do not dismount your horse.
Do not get off your horse,
Taking the black steel saber out of the sack,
Brandish it here and there around the white steppe.
When you cut through the rawhide straps,
Then you will see everything.

If you dismount the horse,
Then you will be bound in the rawhide straps
Undying, you will die,
Immortal, you will perish.

-17-
Hearing this, Chepe Salgyn
Stepped off the golden porch,
Untied his plain chestnut horse,
And clung to him like a bat.
Then, turning the horse away,
He ascended the mountain ridge.
When he reached the mountain ridge,
He pressed the stirrups and spurred the horse:
And so fell upon this earth a black fog
That did not dissipate for nine days!
From here, the rushing horse
Ran and ran,
Did he run a lot, run a little?
In seven gallops
He descended in the embrace of the mountain's saddle
Along the smooth ridge
To the foot of the thundering mountain.
Taking a good look, he sees:
Older-Younger *Shemeldei*-demons
In the white steppe, sitting with their legs crossed.
Chepe Salgyn, entering, so spurred his horse:
That he sank into the midst of the white steppe.
– Come here, Chepe Salgyn, - they said.
He, without dismounting his horse,
Drew the black steel saber,
And began to wave it here and there.
Then he sees:
All the rawhide straps were cut apart.

– *Pai-pai*, Chepe Salgyn, – the *Shemeldei*-demons said, –
You, whose birth filled the white world,
Chepe Salgyn,
Do you truly wish to battle us
Without getting off your horse?
Get off the horse! – so saying,
Older-Younger *Shemeldei*-demons laughed so hard
That the black stone split apart.
When, whooping, they laughed,
The *bogatyr*-cliff began to rock.
Hearing this, Chepe Salgyn,
Did not notice how he jumped from his horse.
And having dismounted his horse, he ran toward them,
And had almost grasped them,
But saw:
Rawhide straps binding him.
At that moment the Older-Younger
Shemeldei-demons approached:
– Wait, Chepe Salgyn! – and they began to threaten, –
Although you are undying, immortal,
How will you escape from us?
Grasping Chepe Salgyn,
They wanted to beat him immediately, however
They could not even lift their right hand.
They grabbed the plain chestnut horse by the bridle.
Having grabbed the plain chestnut hose by the bridle,
They tied Chepe-Salgyn with rawhide straps
To the horse's tail.
Having been tied to the tail,
They dragged him to the black sea.
Having dragged him to the black sea, –
Chepe Salgyn sees –
They had made an iron barrel!
Having made the iron barrel,

They began to shove him into the iron barrel.
Having shoved him into the iron barrel,
They closed the lid,
And pushed it into the black sea.
– Now you will swim away from here, – they said, –
To the place where nine seas flow together, you will swim there,
When you reach the place where nine seas flow together,
You will not escape, you will drown! – so saying,
They shoved the barrel.

-18-

Did he float far, did he float a little?
Suddenly Chepe Salgyn heard,
Someone speaking:
– *Pai-pai*, what is this iron barrel floating here? –
Let me pull the barrel out.
From here, not far to the place,
Where nine seas flow together.
When it floated to him,
This barrel will sink! – so saying,
Someone grasped the iron barrel.
When she grabbed the iron barrel,
She pulled it upstream.
Pulling it onto the hill,
She opened the barrel's lid:
Chepe Salgyn lay there,
Blinking his eyes.
Then he sees:
Kara Shemeldei, who cannot be wrapped
In nine embraces, standing like a mountain:
– *Pai-pai*, Chepe Salgyn, whose birth
Filled the white steppe,
Why are you lying here, bound?
– Do not ask, Kara Shemeldei, – answered Chepe Salgyn,

Searching for you, I traveled the whole white world.
When I arrived on foot at the black mountain
With eighty passes,
I fell victim to Older-Younger
Shemeldei-demons' tricks.
They tossed me, bound, in the barrel,
And pushed me into the black sea.
– Why did you seek me? – asked Kara Shemeldei.
– Why did you seek?
I sought you, glory be your name,
In order to marry you, that is why I sought.
– Are you speaking the truth, Chepe Salgyn?
– Heh, why would I lie?
Hearing this, the Black Shemeldei:
– Ah, these whores,
Look, Older-Younger *Shemeldei*-demons –
Those are my sisters,
With their sixty schemes and plots,
Seventy tricks,
Older-Younger *Shemeldei*-demons.
If you fall victim to them,
They will indeed bind you.
Wait, I will get to you!
Look what they have done
To Chepe Salgyn, whom I will marry!
They wanted to marry you themselves,
And when you denied them,
They used tricks to bind you.
Wait until I get them, – so saying,
She cut apart the rawhide straps.
Using only a knife with a dull edge
She cut them,
Chepe Salgyn jumped up,
And grasped the black *Shemeldei*-demon by her broad breast:

– Wait a moment, descendant of devils,
First I will destroy you! – he said.
– What has come over you, Chepe Salgyn?
You said you sought me in order to marry me?
– Yes, to marry you!
Then, grasping her, he would not permit her to step here or there,
He crumpled her, he grappled her,
And lifted her toward the forty heavens,
Then, turning away, he cast her down
Such that he broke her backbone in nine places.
– That is what you needed! – said he.

-19-
The plain chestnut horse
Had followed him, it turns out.
It now stood nearby.
– Come here, my plain chestnut horse, – he said.
When the plain chestnut horse ran to him,
Chepe Salgyn clung to him like a bat,
And urged him to go higher, to the black mountain.
He drove him and drove him:
He descended in the embrace of the mountain's saddle
Along the smooth ridge
At the foot of the black mountain.
Then he sees:
The Older-Younger *Shemeldei*-demons had stolen
The white livestock and populous village.
Seeing this, behind the white livestock
And the people-village, he descended.
Descended-descended, driving his horse, driving:
Until he reached the entrance-*tyundyuk*.
From there, they drove the people downward.
And he followed them downward.
Down and down –

Beyond the borders of the seventy layers of earth,
Around the world,
Where the black mountain was.
Onto the black mountain, around the other side of the earth,
They drove the white livestock and the people-village.
Seeing this, Chepe Salgyn spurred his horse:
Alongside the Older-Younger
Shemeldei-demons he came down.
Then, leaping off the horse,
He seized both by the collars:
– Wait a minute, *Shemeldei*-demons! – he said. –
You have bound me in rawhide straps with your tricks,
Tossed me into an iron barrel and put me out to sea! – so saying,
He did not allow them to move,
Crumbling them in his grasp,
And lifted them from the black earth,
Turning them, he threw them so hard –
That the ridge was crumbled into nine pieces.
– *Eze*, forty *chaizan*-shepherds, come to me!
Forty *chaizans* ran to him.
– *Eze*, golden *chaizans*,
With your people and livestock,
White livestock, people-village,
Drive them to your land! He said.
– Drive them we will, Chepe Salgyn,
The masters of the home in the white steppe remained.
Eze, Chepe Salgyn, take us to your land, – they said.
– No, golden *chaizans*, – answered Chepe Salgyn, –
If I take you to my land, they will say
"You have brought stolen livestock into the forest!"
Take them to your land,
You, golden *chaizan*,
Your livestock and all the people,
Become a khan, live.

Do you hear, forty *chaizans*? – he said.
– We hear! – they answered.
The golden *chaizan*:
– It that is to be so, so be it! – he agreed.
Turning away, they herded the white livestock.
When they began to herd the white livestock,
Raising their tails, the livestock ran back.
The best of the people,
Shouting and sobbing, began to climb.
Chepe Salgyn turned the horse,
Riding past the white livestock, the people-village,
And then rode onward.

-20-
He rode and rode:
He returned to the white world,
And then drove the horse further onward to his land.
In six gallops
He reached
The white mountain with sixty passes.
Along the smooth ridge,
He descended into the embrace of the mountain's saddle.
Looking closely, he noticed all around:
The people are living as they had lived,
The livestock graze as they have grazed,
And down to the palace, he rode the horse.
Then he saw:
The hinged doors were thrown open,
Tebir Këk ran out:
– Dearest, Chepe Salgyn, whose birth filled the white world,
The man whom I married,
Surely he would not return
Until he had completed everything! – so saying,
She stepped down off the golden porch.

Grasping him by the hand and under the arm,
He dismounted his horse,
And she led him into the golden palace,
She seated him behind the golden table.
When they began to eat and drink,
Tebir Këk said:
– *Eze*, Chepe Salgyn,
How are you?
– How am I? – answered Chepe Salgyn,
I fell for the *Shemeldei*-demons tricks,
And was bound with rawhide straps,
And then they stuffed me into an iron barrel,
And pushed it into the black sea.
As I floated,
Their sister, Kara Shemeldei
Pulled me out and cut the straps.
And I destroyed her pure soul.
When Older-Younger *Shemeldei*-demons
Stole the white livestock and the people-village,
I caught up to them and destroyed their pure souls, – he said.
You father, Kazyr Kan,
And your sisters Kazyr Tek and Tebir Tek
Left the white world.
And I appointed the golden *chaizan*
In place of the khan.
When he and the people asked to come to our land,
I refused to take them into our land.
Let the livestock graze,
Where it has grazed,
Let the people live as they have lived.
– Good, good, my husband, –
Said Tebir Këk,
When they had eaten and drunk,
Chepe Salgyn arose

And walked out of the golden palace,
– Ah, it turns out his father had died.
When he died, they laid him to rest:
After nine days they built a coffin,
And hung it upright.
Altyn Aryg, his mother, is still living.

-21-
Chepe Salgyn left the golden palace,
Took the saddle off the plain chestnut horse.
Removing the bridle from the horse's head, he said:
– *Eze*, my plain chestnut horse,
Go to *Syuryun* Mountain,
And there, nibbling, eat grass.
When you reach the milk lake,
Drink water there.
When I need to call you, I will whistle,
Come to me, – and so saying,
And he smacked the plain chestnut horse's smooth rump,
And set him free.
When the plain chestnut horse galloped off,
He went into the golden palace,
And sat behind the golden table.
He became a great khan among khans,
A great *piy*-leader among leaders.
They grew rich and lived well.
No strange men come shouting into their land,
Bringing them to bay, no war comes.
And thus, richly, they lived happily ever after.

List of Characters

In Shor and English

Hero Legends
АЛЫПТЫҒ НЫБАҚТАР

1. Chepe Salgyn and his Plain Chestnut Horse
Чепе Салгын, имеющий неказистого рыжего коня

Female names

Altyn Aryg	'Golden Pure'	Алтын Арыг
Altyn Kas or	'Golden Goose'	Алтын Қас
Altyn Chüstük	'Golden Signet Ring'	Алтын Чўстўк
Kazyr/Tebir Kĕk	'Terrible Cuckoo'	Қазыр Кööк
Kara Shemeldei	'Black Demon'	Қара Шемелдей
Kydai Aryg	'China Purity'	Қыдай/Қыдат Арыг
Ches Shemeldei	'Copper Demon'	Чес Шемельдей

Male names

Ak Kan	'White Khan'	Ак Қаан
Altyn Kylysh	'White Saber or Sword'	Алтын Қылыш
Kazyr Kan	'Terrible Khan' or 'Fast Khan'	Қазыр Каан
Kazyr Tek	'Terrible Hook'	Қазыр Тек
Kara Alyp	'Black Alyp'[23]	Қара Алып
Tebir Tek	'Iron Hook'	Тебир Тек
Chepe Salgyn	'Plain Wind'	Чеппе Салғын

2. Kĕk Torchuk

Кĕк Торчук

Female characters

Ay Kĕk	'Lunar cuckoo'	Ай Кööк
Alak Manak	'Spotted Chinese'[24]	Ала Манык
Ak Kĕzhee	'White Obelisk'/'White Stella'	Ак Кöжеге
Kĕk Torgu	'Blue Silk'	Кöк Торгу
Kyun Aryg	'Sunny Purity'/'Sunny Pure'	Кÿн Арыг

Male characters

Ay Kan	'Lunar Khan'	Ай Қаан
Ak Kan	'White Khan'	Ак Қаан
Altyn Tas	'Golden Bald Man'	Алтын Тас
Altyn Shur	'Golden Coral'/'Golden Bead'	Алтын Шур
Kara Kaia	'Black Cliff'	Қара Қайа
Kara Kan Mergen	'Black Khan-Arrow'	Қара Қаан Мерген
Kara Kazan	'Black Pot'	Қара Қазан
Kara Salgyn	'Black Wind'	Қара Салгын
Kara Turtus	'Black Warrior'	Қара Туртус
Kara Shoyun	'Black Iron Ore'	Қара Шойун
Kan Mergen	'Khan Arrow'	Қаан Мерген
Kĕk Kan	'Blue Khan'	Кöк Қаан
Kĕk Torchuk	'Blue Nightingale'	Кöк Торчук
Kuba Salgyn	'Light Wind'	Куба Салгын
Kyun Kan	'Sunny Khan'	Кÿн Қаан
Kyuren Kylysh	'Brown Saber'/'Brown Sword'	Кÿрен Қылыш

Shor-English Glossary

Abo – *або* – interjection, cry expressing sadness, dissatisfaction, surprise, etc.

Adanmada – адаңмада – interjection denoting extreme ecstasy or horror

Aina or *shaman* – *айна* – devil (in Shor tales, a devil has large ears, fangs, and a tail), evil spirit, demon

Alyp – *Алып* – bogatyr, clan or tribal leader

Bogatyr, bogatyrka – богатыр (male), *богатырка* (female) – Russian term for a mythical hero warrior or leader

Chaian, Chaiachy – *Чайан, Чайачы* – Creator, deity of the Upper World

Chaizan – *Чайзаң* – Herder, steward

Che – *Че* – 'Yes', word expressing an affirmative reply, agreement

Chegen - *Чеген* – Atmosphere, air, envelope of air around the earth. In the phrase *'chegen tübü'* it is understood to mean 'bottom of the earth'.

Eze – *Эзе* – 1. Word expressing agreement ('yes'); 2. Introductory word denoting firm confidence in the accuracy, truth of a statement ('certainly', 'doubtlessly', 'indisputably'). 3. Particle meaning energetic affirmation, agreement ('yes', 'certainly', undoubtedly', 'absolutely'). 4. Particle often used at the start of an utterance to show that the next statement is the result of deep consideration by the storyteller or is of a general nature. 5. Interjection expressing various speech nuances (affirmation, contemplation, speaking to a conversation partner).

Kan – *қаан* – khan, tribal or state leader

Kudai – Кудай – Deity of the Upper World, god

Kurumnik, kuruma – *Курỳмник, курума* – (Russian) Loose rock deposits on slope or level mountainous surface that slowly slide downward ('stone rivers' and 'stone seas'). Sometimes a kuruma can be covered in vegetation and in other cases water may flow below the stones. Kurumniks are the result of ice weathering of mountain soils in a high altitude climate.

Pai-pai – *Пай-пай* – Interjection expressing surprise

Piy – *Пий* – 1. Well-known, wealthy person; 2. Leader of a tribe or clan; 3. Judge in a clan or tribal unit, not elected but acknowledged by the people

Syuryum, syurgyu – *Сӱрӱм, Сӱргӱ* – Name of a mythological mountain at the center of the world

Tashaor – *Ташаор* – leather container for storing alcoholic beverages

Taskyl – *Тасқыл* – Naked mountain peak covered in ice

Tastar – *Тастар* – Bald man (usually to describe herders)

Tundyuk – *Тундюк, тӱндӱк* – smoke flap, chimney, pipe; here used to mean 'entrance to the Underworld'

Place Names

Syurgyum or Syurgyu – *Сӱргӱм /Сӱргӱ* – Mythological mountain at the center of the world

Chernaya Non-Gora – *Черная Нон-гора* – Mythological "Mount Black" located in the Underworld

Endnotes

1. Transl. note – Male *Bogatyr* or female *bogatyrka* is the Russian term for 'epic hero'.

2. Transl. note – The same is true for the Russian to English translation.

3. 'Bogatyr' (male), 'bogatyrka' (female) and 'alyp' are, respectively, Russian and Shor terms for a warrior, hero figure, often legendary or mythical.

4. Metaphor meaning to rescue or save an *alyp* from unavoidable death.

5. Remark by the storyteller.

6. Remark by the storyteller.

7. *Tyundyuk* is a round wooden rim frame with a grid that is installed in the top center of a yurt or ger for ventilation.

8. 1 sazhen = 7 feet, an obsolete Russian unit of measurement

9. Transl. – 'Yes' in Shor.

10. The god threw a magical egg down to Earth to help the old and childless *alyp*. The boy sprang from the egg.

11. Used in epic poetry to describe a long, exhausting journey.

12. Remark by the narrator.

13. Remark to the listener-story gatherer (L.N. Arbachakova).

14. 1 sazhen = 7 feet, an obsolete Russian measurement

15. Storyteller speaks to attest to his presence in the epic world.

16. Said figuratively of a person who has lived to see grandchildren.

17. 'Bogatyr' (male) 'bogatyrka' (female) and 'alyp' are, respectively, Russian and Shor terms for a warrior, knight-errant, strong person, often legendary or mythical.

18. The cosmic worldview of the Shor people, like other Turkic peoples in Siberia, is vertical in structure: Upper, Middle, and Lower Worlds.

19. A clan's mountain, forbidden for entry by non-clan members. It is a border between the khan's land possessions and other lands.

20. *Tyundyuk* is a round wooden rim frame with a grid that is installed in the top center of a yurt to allow for ventilation.
21. Storyteller-*kaichi* remark indicating his presence in the epic world.
22. A common epic phrase to describe the beauty of heroes.
23. 'Bogatyr' or 'hero warrior'.
24. Name of the best Chinese silk.

PAGANISM & SHAMANISM

What is Paganism? A religion, a spirituality, an alternative belief system, nature worship? You can find support for all these definitions (and many more) in dictionaries, encyclopaedias, and text books of religion, but subscribe to any one and the truth will evade you. Above all Paganism is a creative pursuit, an encounter with reality, an exploration of meaning and an expression of the soul. Druids, Heathens, Wiccans and others, all contribute their insights and literary riches to the Pagan tradition. Moon Books invites you to begin or to deepen your own encounter, right here, right now.

If you have enjoyed this book, why not tell other readers by posting a review on your preferred book site.

Recent bestsellers from Moon Books are:

Journey to the Dark Goddess
How to Return to Your Soul
Jane Meredith
Discover the powerful secrets of the Dark Goddess and transform your depression, grief and pain into healing and integration.
Paperback: 978-1-84694-677-6 ebook: 978-1-78099-223-5

Shamanic Reiki
Expanded Ways of Working with Universal Life Force Energy
Llyn Roberts, Robert Levy
Shamanism and Reiki are each powerful ways of healing; together,

their power multiplies. *Shamanic Reiki* introduces techniques to help healers and Reiki practitioners tap ancient healing wisdom.
Paperback: 978-1-84694-037-8 ebook: 978-1-84694-650-9

Pagan Portals – The Awen Alone
Walking the Path of the Solitary Druid
Joanna van der Hoeven
An introductory guide for the solitary Druid, *The Awen Alone* will accompany you as you explore, and seek out your own place within the natural world.
Paperback: 978-1-78279-547-6 ebook: 978-1-78279-546-9

A Kitchen Witch's World of Magical Herbs & Plants
Rachel Patterson
A journey into the magical world of herbs and plants, filled with magical uses, folklore, history and practical magic. By popular writer, blogger and kitchen witch, Tansy Firedragon.
Paperback: 978-1-78279-621-3 ebook: 978-1-78279-620-6

Medicine for the Soul
The Complete Book of Shamanic Healing
Ross Heaven
All you will ever need to know about shamanic healing and how to become your own shaman…
Paperback: 978-1-78099-419-2 ebook: 978-1-78099-420-8

Shaman Pathways – The Druid Shaman
Exploring the Celtic Otherworld
Danu Forest
A practical guide to Celtic shamanism with exercises and techniques as well as traditional lore for exploring the Celtic Otherworld.
Paperback: 978-1-78099-615-8 ebook: 978-1-78099-616-5